D1560461

❖ 49 ❖
Easy Electronic Projects for the 556 Dual Timer

❖ 49 ❖
Easy Electronic Projects for the 556 Dual Timer

Delton T. Horn

TAB **TAB BOOKS**

Blue Ridge Summit, PA

FIRST EDITION
FIRST PRINTING

© 1991 by **TAB BOOKS**.
TAB BOOKS is a division of McGraw-Hill, Inc.

Library of Congress Cataloging-in-Publication Data

Horn, Delton T.
    49 easy electronic projects for the 556 dual timer / by Delton T.
Horn.
        p.   cm.
    Includes index.
    ISBN 0-8306-7454-3   ISBN 0-8306-3454-1 (pbk.)
    1. Multivibrators—Amateurs' manuals. I. Title. II. Title:
Forty-nine easy electronic projects for the 556 dual timer.
III. Title: Dual timer.
TK9965.H63   1990
621.381—dc20   90-22549
                                                    CIP

TAB BOOKS offers software for sale. For information and a catalog, please contact TAB Software Department, Blue Ridge Summit, PA 17294-0850.

Questions regarding the content of this book should be addressed to:

Reader Inquiry Branch
TAB BOOKS
Blue Ridge Summit, PA 17294-0850

Acquisitions Editor: Roland S. Phelps
Technical Editor: Steven L. Burwen
Production: Katherine G. Brown
Book Design: Jaclyn J. Boone
Cover Design: Lori E. Schlosser

Contents

Introduction

THE 555 TIMER IS ONE OF THE MOST POPULAR ICS ON THE MARKET TODAY. A number of books have been written on this chip and its many applications.

This book is a bit different. It concentrates on the 555's "big brother," the 556 dual-timer IC, which contains two independent 555-type timers in a single package. Two timers are twice as powerful as just one, opening up many possibilities for more sophisticated applications.

Of course, two separate 555 ICs could be used, but this is a little inelegant when the 556 offers a more convenient approach to constructing the projects.

Forty-nine practical projects for the 556 dual-timer IC are featured in this book, divided into four basic categories;

- Timers
- Signal generators
- LED displays
- Miscellaneous

I'm sure you'll find a number of interesting, useful, and exciting projects in this book. The 556 dual-timer IC is such a versatile device that the 49 projects in this book just barely scratch the surface of its potential applications.

❖ 1
The 556
and its relatives

THE 556 IS A DUAL-TIMER IC; THAT IS, IT CONTAINS TWO COMPLETE AND independent timer sections in a single package. Both sections are identical. The only pins common to both sections are the supply voltage (pin #14) and ground (pin #7). All other functions are brought out individually.

Each timer section has six pins of its own:

- Discharge
- Threshold
- Control voltage
- Reset
- Output
- Trigger

I will discuss the functions controlled by each of these pins later in this chapter.

Because there are 6 pins for each of 2 timer sections, plus 2 common power-supply pins, this chip has a total of 14 pins.

MULTIVIBRATORS

A timer circuit has two possible output states: high and low. After a specific preset period of time, the timer's output reverses states. A timer is a form of a type of circuit known as a *multivibrator*.

All multivibrators have two possible output states: high and low. There are three basic types of multivibrator circuits:

- Monostable multivibrator
- Bistable multivibrator
- Astable multivibrator

The differences among the three types of multivibrators lie in how the output switches states.

A *monostable multivibrator* has one stable output state, which can be either high or low, depending on the specific circuit design used. For the sake of discussion, assume the stable output state is low. This stable state normally will be held as long as power is applied to the circuit. The only way to get the multivibrator's output to jump to the opposite, nonstable state (high) is to feed in an appropriate trigger pulse.

Once a suitable trigger pulse has been detected by the circuit, the monostable multivibrator's output jumps to its nonstable state (high) for a specific, preset period of time. Once the circuit has timed out, the output reverts to its normal, stable state.

A *bistable multivibrator* has two stable states. The output can be held either high or low indefinitely, as long as power is applied continuously to the circuit. The output reverses states each time a suitable trigger pulse is received at the input. Timers are not used in bistable multivibrator circuits. This type of multivibrator is mentioned here only for the sake of completeness.

The third type of multivibrator circuit is the *astable multivibrator*, which has no stable output states. Neither the high state nor the low state can be held past a specific preset period of time. As long as power is applied to an astable multivibrator circuit, the output state keeps switching back and forth at a rate determined by various component values within the circuit. No external trigger pulse is required for an astable multivibrator circuit to switch its output state.

Timers, such as those within the 556 dual-timer IC, are used commonly in monostable multivibrator and astable multivibrator applications. A timer chip such as the 556 is not suitable for use in bistable multivibrator circuits.

I discuss practical monostable multivibrator and astable multivibrator circuits later in this chapter. Practical applications for such circuits will make up the bulk of the rest of this book.

THE 556 AND THE 555

Each of the two timer sections in the 556 IC are identical to the timer used in the 555 IC. Essentially, the 556 is a pair of 555 chips in a single housing, with the power-supply connections internally hard-wired together.

The 555 timer IC is one of the most popular and versatile of all integrated circuits currently available to the electronics hobbyist. The two-in-one 556 is obviously twice as powerful.

Because it is convenient to look at just one timer section (they are both identical), the discussion begins with an in-depth examination of the 555 timer IC.

THE INTERNAL STRUCTURE OF THE 555

The 555 timer is certainly one of the most popular integrated circuits of all time. This readily available and inexpensive chip can be used in countless timing applications. It offers high reliability, ease of use, and reasonable precision at low cost. Circuit designs built around the 555 timer are usually fairly simple and straightforward.

Although there are some occasional exceptions, the 555 timer normally is supplied in an 8-pin DIP case, as shown in Fig. 1-1. A simplified diagram of the 555 timer's internal circuitry appears in Fig. 1-2. We will be referring back to these two diagrams throughout this section.

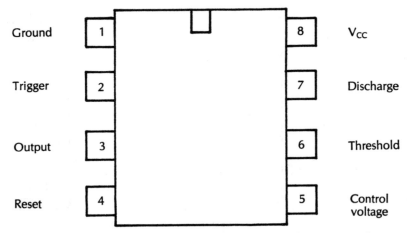

Fig. 1-1 *The 555 timer is one of the most popular ICs around.*

We will now examine the functions of each of the 555's eight pins.

Pin 1: Ground   This is the connection point for the negative end of the power supply and the circuit ground (or common). The voltage on this pin should be the lowest (most negative) voltage applied to any of the 555's pins. For most applications, the voltage on this pin will be true ground, or 0 volts (V). No more negative voltage should ever be applied to any of the chip's other pins.

Pin 2: Trigger   This pin is used to initiate a timing cycle. It feeds into the lower comparator stage (see Fig. 1-2), and when the voltage on this pin is sufficiently large, it sets the latch. This forces the output to go to its high state.

The trigger input normally is held high. To trigger the timer, the voltage on pin #2 must drop to a value less than one-third of the circuit's supply voltage (V +). This often (though not always) will be about one-half the voltage appearing at pin #5.

The 555's trigger input is level sensitive. The input signal does not

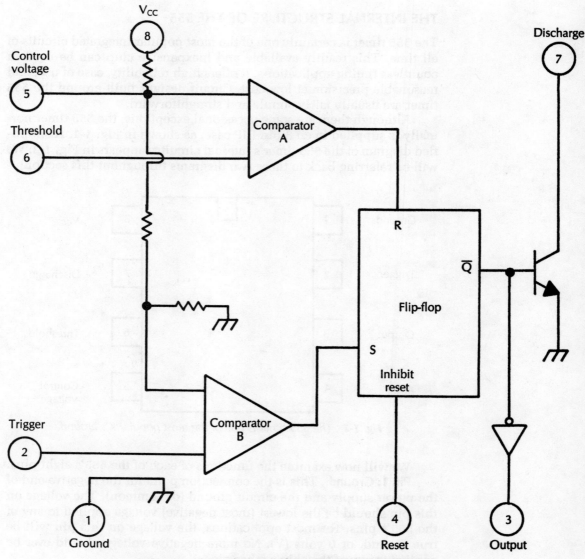

Fig. 1-2 *This is the internal circuitry of the 555 timer IC.*

necessarily have to be a sharp pulse. A slowly changing waveform (such as a sine wave, or ramp wave) also can be used to trigger the timer.

For proper operation, the trigger input should not be held in the low state. If the trigger signal is less than $1/3$ V + for a period longer than the circuit's timing cycle, the timer will be retriggered automatically as soon as it times out. At the other extreme, the trigger signal should go low for at least 1 μS (microsecond) to trigger the timer circuit reliably.

Because of delays within the 555's internal circuitry, the output timing period should be at least 10 μS to prevent possible retriggering with a 1 μS trigger pulse. In most practical hobbyist applications, you will be dealing with output timing cycles considerably longer than 10 μS, so the few microseconds of internal delay within the chip itself will be negligible and can safely be ignored.

The voltage applied to the trigger input (pin #2) should never be higher than the voltage at pin #8 (V +) or lower than the voltage at pin #1 (ground).

A dc current (usually called the trigger current) flows from the 555's pin #2 into the external circuit. The value of this current sets the maximum permissible resistance between pin #2 and ground. The trigger current is typically about 500 nA. For a supply voltage of + 5 V, the resistance between pin #2 and ground can be as high as 3 megohms (3 million ohms). Increasing the circuit's supply voltage also increases the maximum allowable resistance. This maximum resistance affects the maximum possible timing period, as you will see shortly.

Pin 3: Output   The timer's output pulse normally is taken from this pin. The output is normally low and goes high only during the timing cycle initiated by the trigger signal at pin #2.

The output signal is passed through a series of high-current, totempoled transistors. In the low (normal) state, the output voltage is essentially at ground potential (0 volts). During the timing cycle, the timer's output goes high, with a voltage that is approximately 1.7 volts less than the circuit's supply voltage.

The output of the 555 timer can be made compatible with most digital logic families, such as TTL or CMOS. The circuit's supply voltage should be selected to suit the digital devices. For low-state loads referenced to the V + rail (TTL gates are an example), the 555's output is designed for appropriate current sinking.

The output signal at pin #3 is always in a state opposite to the 555's internal latch. Because of this, the trigger input (pin #2) normally is held high (low output) and drops to a low state to initiate a timing cycle (high output).

The switching rate between the low and high output conditions is very fast and is usually negligible for practical applications. For convenience, you can assume that the timer's output can switch instantaneously between the low and high output states. Actually, there is a brief transistion time between states. The transistion time can be reasonably ignored in virtually all hobbyist applications.

Pin 4: Reset   An appropriate signal on pin #4 resets the timer, aborting the timing cycle. When pin #4 is activated, the 555's internal latch is reset to a high state, and the timer's output reverts to its normal low state.

The pulse at the reset pin (pin #4) must last at least 0.5 μS to reset the timer reliably. The effect is not instantaneous. Typically, there will be a delay of approximately 0.5 μS after the reset pulse before the device is reset.

The reset voltage threshold level is 0.7 volt. The reset signal must supply at least 0.1 mA to reset the timer reliably. Unlike most of the other signals described in this section, these required voltages and currents are independent of the circuit's supply voltage. One benefit of this is that an output signal from a TTL gate can be used to reset the 555 timer, no matter what supply voltage is being used for the timer circuit.

In many practical applications, the reset input is not used. In such circuits, pin #4 should be shorted to the V + supply voltage rail to prevent possible false resetting. Most 555 timer applications do not use the reset pin, although it comes in handy in applications in which the timing cycle might have to be stopped prematurely before the timer times out.

Pin 5: Control voltage   Pin #5 is another pin included in the 555 for special purposes, but it is not used in the most practical applications.

Referring to the 555's internal circuitry diagram in Fig. 1-2, you can see that pin #5 permits direct access to the voltage divider at the $^2/_3$-V + point. This is the reference voltage for the upper comparator stage. By inserting an external voltage at this point, you can affect the internal switching points, and thus, the timing of the circuit. Thus, pin #5 offers voltage control of the timing cycle.

Generally speaking, the functional voltage-control range runs from about 2 volts above ground value at pin #1 up to one volt less than the V + voltage at pin #8. This range is not guaranteed by the manufacturer. Usually, voltages outside this range can be applied without damaging the chip, but to ensure reliability, it is strongly advised that the voltage-control input never be permitted to exceed the V + voltage or drop below ground potential (as defined by pin #1).

In most practical timer applications, the voltage control input (pin #5) is not used. Generally, it can be left floating, but this could cause some stability problems in some circuits. To make the timer circuit more immune to noise, it is a good idea to bypass pin #5 (when it is not being used) to ground through a small capacitor. A good value for this is 0.01 μF (1μF = 0.000001 farad). This bypass capacitor is not always essential, but it is advisable. It is good, cheap insurance against possible stability problems. It does not add appreciably to the cost of the circuit. I make it a general practice always to include a bypass capacitor in any timer circuit that does not use the voltage-control input. I don't worry about whether or not it is necessary in that particular circuit. It certainly isn't going to do any harm, and it might help. I feel my time is worth more than the cost of the bypass capacitor. By always using the bypass capacitor, I don't have to waste any time determining if such a capacitor is required.

If you insist, you can experiment with omitting the voltage-control bypass capacitor in the projects presented throughout this book, but, personally, I don't see much point in such experimentation. If you are ever working with a timer circuit without a voltage-control bypass capacitor, and the circuit does not seem to be functioning properly, try adding a bypass capacitor to the circuit. This practice often clears up the problem immediately.

There is no real point in experimenting with different values for the bypass capacitor. A $0.01\text{-}\mu F$ capacitor will do the job just fine. Changing the value will not affect the operation of the circuit.

Pin 6: Threshold   The input signal at pin #6 is fed to the upper comparator stage (see Fig. 1-2). This voltage is compared to the $2/3$ V + value set by the internal voltage divider and any input voltage at pin #5. The output of this comparator stage is used to reset the latch, bringing the timer's output back to its normal low state at the conclusion of the timing cycle.

The threshold input (pin #6) is normally held low (below two-thirds of the circuit's supply voltage). Bringing this input high (above two-thirds of the circuit's supply voltage) activates the resetting procedure.

This threshold input (pin #6) is level sensitive. A sharp input pulse is not required. A slowly changing waveform such as a sine wave or a ramp wave will work just as well, as long as it passes through the critical voltage value ($2/3$ V +).

The voltage applied to pin #4 should never be permitted to exceed the circuit's supply voltage (V + at pin #8) or drop below the ground value (at pin #1). This input draws a dc threshold current from the input source that determines the maximum resistance that can appear between pin #6 and the positive supply-voltage rail (V +). This threshold current is typically about 100 nA. There might be some slight fluctuation from unit to unit, but the differences generally will be negligible for hobbyist applications.

Assuming that the timer's supply voltage is + 5 volts, the resistance between pin #6 and the V + supply rail is 16 megohms. If a larger supply voltage is used in the circuit, the maximum resistance also can be increased. This maximum resistance affects the maximum possible timing period, as we will see shortly.

Pin 7: Discharge   The discharge pin (#7) is the open collector of an on-chip npn transistor used to clamp the appropriate nodes of the timing network to ground. In most practical circuits, a timing capacitor is connected between pin #7 and ground.

The npn transistor at pin #7 operates in tandem with the timer's output (pin #3). When the timer's output is low, the discharge transistor will be on. The internal resistance from pin #7 to ground (pin #1) will be a fairly small value. Similarly, when the timer's output is high, the discharge transistor will be cut off. There will now be a fairly large resistance from pin #7 to ground (pin #1).

In some special applications, the discharge terminal (pin #7) can be used as an auxiliary output terminal. This secondary output exhibits much the same current-sinking capability as the main output (pin #3).

Pin 8: V +   Pin #8 is the 555's positive power-supply terminal. The highest (most positive) voltage applied to any of the chip's pins should be fed into this terminal.

The 555 timer is quite flexible in its power-supply requirements. It will accept a supply voltage as low as + 4.5 V and as high as + 16 V. These limits should not be exceeded or erratic operation could result, or the IC itself might be permanently damaged. Most manufacturer's recommend a practical power-supply range of + 5 V to + 15 V. Generally speaking, a supply voltage in the range of + 9 V to + 12 V probably will be the best choice for most applications.

If a + 5-volt power supply is used, the 555 can be interfaced directly with TTL gates and similar digital circuitry. This timer chip is also fully compatible with digital CMOS devices.

The 555 timer's operation is relatively independent of the supply voltage used. For most practical hobbyist applications, the timing period of the circuit is not affected noticeably by changes in the supply voltage. The sensitivity to power-supply fluctuations typically is rated at 0.1% per volt. That is, if the circuit is set up for a time period of 500 seconds, a 2-volt drop in the supply voltage would only change the timing period to 499 seconds. This is a negligible difference for the vast majority of practical applications. Component tolerances are likely to account for at least this much error.

The most significant result of changing the 555 timer's supply voltage is in the output drive capability. Both the available output current and the output voltage increase as the supply voltage is increased. This can be important if the timer is to drive a large, power-hungry load.

The 555 timer is used normally in either the monostable or the astable mode. I explained these terms earlier in this chapter, when multivibrators were introduced. In either mode, the timing period is set up by external resistor/capacitor combinations, according to fairly simple formulae. Overall, this timer is quite easy to use.

THE 555 MONOSTABLE MULTIVIBRATOR CIRCUIT

The monostable multivibrator often is known by several alternate names. Some of the most popular include:

- Timer
- Time delay
- One-shot
- Pulse stretcher

I think that calling a monostable multivibrator a *timer circuit* is somewhat misleading, since many (though certainly not all) monostable multivibrator circuits are built around timer ICs, which also are used for other purposes. Yes, a monostable multivibrator serves a timing function, but it is easy to get confused by calling it a *timer circuit.*

The term *time delay* gives a good indication of the operation of a monostable multivibrator. The output pulse ends some time after the input (trigger) pulse.

The name *one-shot* also describes the functioning of this type of circuit. There is one output pulse for each input (trigger) pulse.

Because the output pulse must always be longer than the input (trigger) pulse, the term *pulse stretcher* is also an appropriate description of a monostable multivibrator.

In some technical literature, different names are used for the same basic circuitry, depending on the intended application.

Figure 1-3 illustrates the operation of a typical monostable multivibrator circuit. Note that the length of the output pulse is not related to the length of the input (trigger) pulse.

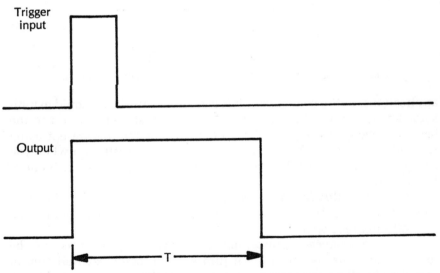

Fig. 1-3 *A monostable multivibrator generates a fixed-length output pulse for each trigger pulse at its input.*

The basic 555 monostable multivibrator circuit appears in Fig. 1-4. Note how simple this circuit is. There are just three external components besides the 555 timer IC itself: two capacitors and a single resistor. Resistor R1 and capacitor C1 control the timing period of the circuit. I will discuss these components in some detail shortly.

Capacitor C2 is a simple bypass capacitor for the unused voltage-control input (pin #5). This bypass capacitor will not be needed in all

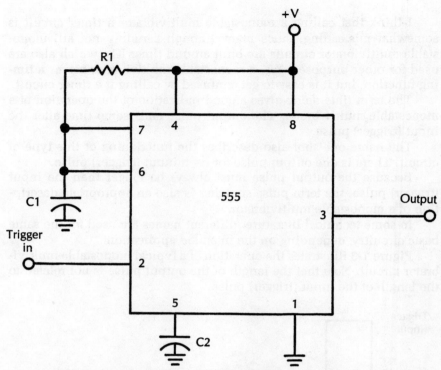

Fig. 1-4 *This is the basic 555 monostable multivibrator circuit.*

applications, but in some cases, if it is not used, the timer could exhibit some stability problems. I'd strongly advise that you always use the bypass capacitor in any 555 timer circuit whenever you are not using the voltage-control input. It could save you some frustration when you run across a circuit that decides to act up. The bypass capacitor is cheap insurance.

A typical value for the bypass capacitor (C2) is 0.01 μF. The exact value is not at all critical. Changing the capacitor value will not noticeably affect circuit operation.

In some advanced applications, an external signal source will be fed into the voltage-control input (pin #5) to provide external control over the circuit's timing period. Of course, if the voltage-control input is being used, the bypass capacitor (C2) should be omitted from the circuitry.

A negative-going trigger pulse is fed into pin #2 of the 555 timer IC. The signal on this pin normally should be high, going low when a timing cycle is to be initiated. This trigger pulse must be shorter than the desired output pulse to avoid immediate retriggering of the timer. For more information on the requirements of the trigger signal for the 555 timer, refer back to the discussion of pin #2 presented earlier in this chapter.

The monostable multivibrator's output is the output pin of the timer IC (pin #3). This output signal normally will be low. When the timer is triggered, the output signal will go high for a specific period of time determined by resistor R1 and capacitor C1. After the circuit times out, the output goes low again and waits for the next incoming trigger pulse.

The formula for the timing cycle in this 555 monostable multivibrator circuit is fairly simple:

$$T = 1.1\, R_1 C_1$$

1.1 is a constant resulting from the circuit design within the 555 timer itself. R_1 is the resistance of the timing resistor in ohms, and C_1 is the capacitance of the timing capacitor in farads.

In some cases, it might be more convenient to convert the resistance to megohms and the capacitance to microfarads. This will give the same results. Just be careful not to get mixed up and try to combine megohms with farads or ohms with microfarads. For the sake of consistency, ohms and farads will be used in the equations throughout this book.

To get a good feel of the workings of this 555 monostable multivibrator circuit, let's run through a few quick examples. First, let's assume that you are using the following component values:

$$R_1 = 220\text{ k}\Omega$$
$$C_1 = 0.5\ \mu\text{F}$$

In this case, the timing period of the monostable multivibrator circuit works out to:

$$T = 1.1 \times 220{,}000 \times 0.0000005$$
$$= 0.121 \text{ second}$$

For the next example, let's see what happens if you increase the capacitance without changing the resistance:

$$R_1 = 220\text{ k}\Omega$$
$$C_1 = 33\ \mu\text{F}$$
$$T = 1.1 \times 220{,}000 \times 0.000033$$
$$= 7.986 \text{ seconds}$$
$$\approx 8 \text{ seconds}$$

Increasing the timing capacitance increases the timing period.

Next, let's keep the same value for the capacitor (C1), but give resistor R1 a larger value:

$$R_1 = 3.3\text{ M}\Omega$$
$$C_1 = 33\ \mu\text{F}$$
$$T = 1.1 \times 3{,}300{,}000 \times 0.000033$$
$$= 119.79 \text{ seconds}$$
$$\approx 2 \text{ minutes}$$

Increasing the value of either the timing capacitor or the timing resistor (or both) increases the timing period. Similarly, decreasing either (or both) of these component values produces a shorter timing period for the circuit.

The 555 timer IC can cover quite a remarkable range of timing values, especially considering its small size, low cost, and ease of use. For reliable operation, the values of the timing components (capacitor C1 and resistor R1) should be kept within certain limits, which still leaves a very wide range.

Timing capacitor C1 should be no smaller than 100 pF and no larger than 1000 μF. Similarly, the minimum value for resistor R1 is 10 kΩ, and the maximum resistance value is 14 MΩ.

To see how this affects the timing range, let's quickly calculate the timing period for both the minimum and the maximum component values. First, let's see what timing period results when both timing components are at their minimum acceptable values:

$$R_1 = 10 \text{ k}\Omega$$
$$C_1 = 100 \text{ pF}$$
$$T = 1.1 \times 10,000 \times 0.0000000001$$
$$= 0.0000011 \text{ second}$$
$$= 1.1 \text{ microseconds}$$

Now, let's give both timing components their maximum acceptable values and see how the circuit's timing period works out:

$$R_1 = 14 \text{ M}\Omega$$
$$C_1 = 1000 \text{ }\mu\text{F}$$
$$T = 1.1 \times 14,000,000 \times 0.001$$
$$= 15,400 \text{ seconds}$$
$$= 256 \text{ minutes, 40 seconds}$$
$$= 4 \text{ hours, 16 minutes, 40 seconds}$$

From just over 1 microsecond to over 4¼ hours is quite an impressive range! This range should cover the vast majority of hobbyist applications.

When longer timing periods are required, multiple monostable multivibrator stages can be *cascaded*; that is, when one times out, it triggers the next timer in line, extending the delay at the circuit's final output. Of course, the 556 dual-timer IC comes in very handy for such multistage applications.

In most practical circuit-design applications, you will know the desired timing period, but you will need to determine the appropriate values for the timing components (resistor R1 and capacitor C1). It is an easy enough matter to rearrange algebraically the basic timing equation to accomplish this.

In most cases, it is more practical to start off by arbitrarily selecting a likely value for capacitor C1, and then solving for resistor R1. As a general rule of thumb, resistors are readily available in more discrete values than capacitors. If the calculated value for resistor R1 is not close to a standard resistor value, multiple resistors can be combined in series and/or parallel combinations to make up the required resistance value. In applications demanding greater precision, a potentiometer or trimpot can be used for R1 to permit fine tuning of the circuit's timing period. A potentiometer also permits continuous manual control over the circuit's timing period, even during operation of the monostable multivibrator.

Occasionally, especially if you haven't much experience working with 555 timer circuits, you will end up with an awkward or out of range (less than 10 kΩ, or greater than 14 MΩ) value for resistor R1. If this happens, just select a new value for capacitor C1, and try again. As you gain familiarity with this circuit, you will find it fairly easy to select an appropriate capacitance value.

Rearranging the basic timing equation to solve for an unknown resistance (R_1), you obtain this new, modified formula:

$$T = 1.1 R_1 C_1$$
$$= \frac{T}{1.1 C_1} = \frac{1.1 R_1 C_1}{1.1 R_1 C_1}$$
$$= \frac{T}{1.1 C_1} = R_1$$
$$R_1 = \frac{T}{1.1 C_1}$$

Let's see how this works out with a specific example. You can assume that you need a monostable multivibrator circuit with a timing period of 17 seconds. This is a moderately long timing period, so you will probably need a fairly large capacitor. Let's try a 50-μF capacitor for C1.

Now it's just a matter of plugging the time and capacitance values into the rearranged equation:

$$R_1 = \frac{17}{1.1 \times 0.00005}$$
$$= \frac{17}{0.000055}$$
$$= 309,091 \text{ ohms}$$

If the intended application is not particularly critical, you can use either a 330-kΩ or a 270-kΩ resistor for R1. These are the closest standard resistor values. If you used a 330-kΩ resistor, the nominal timing period would be changed to:

$$T = 1.1 \times 330,000 \times 0.00005$$
$$= 18.15 \text{ seconds}$$

The component tolerances are likely to introduce at least this much error.

In an application demanding higher precision, try using a 270-kΩ resistor in series with a 50 kΩ or a 100-kΩ potentiometer for R1. This allows the circuit operator to adjust precisely the resistance for the desired timing period and even compensate for any inaccuracies in the capacitor's nominal value.

To further illustrate the circuit design process, assume that the calculated resistor value in the last example (309,091 ohms) just isn't close enough. In such a case, you can throw out your calculations, substitute a new capacitor value, and try again. This time try a 100-μF capacitor for C1. This changes the required value of resistor R1 to:

$$R_1 = \frac{17}{1.1 \times 0.0001}$$
$$= \frac{17}{0.00011}$$
$$= 154,545 \text{ ohms}$$

A standard 150-kΩ resistor would be very close to this calculated value.

The 555 timer IC is designed to be triggered from a negative-going pulse. In some applications, you might need to use a positive-going pulse to initiate the monostable multivibrator's timing cycle. All that is

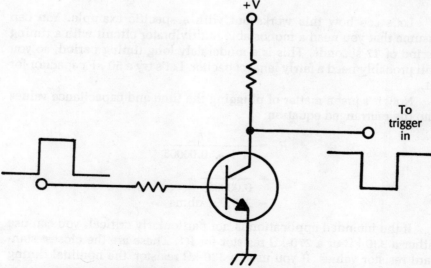

Fig. 1-5 Some applications require the polarity of the trigger pulse to be inverted.

needed is a simple polarity inverter, such as the circuit shown in Fig. 1-5. Almost any npn transistor can be used in this application. The requirements are very loose, and it is more than likely that any npn transistor you happen to have handy will do the job just fine.

THE 555 ASTABLE MULTIVIBRATOR CIRCUIT

The 555 timer IC also can be used in the astable mode. An astable multivibrator, you should recall, has no stable output states. As long as power is applied to the circuit, the output continuously switches back and forth between the low and high states at a regular rate. The low time and the high time are not necessarily equal. No external trigger source is required. An astable multivibrator circuit is self-triggering.

The output of a typical astable multivibrator circuit appears in Fig. 1-6. This is obviously a repeating (or periodic) ac waveform. Because of the boxy shape of the signal, it is called a *rectangle wave*. Sometimes the term *pulse wave* is used instead of rectangle wave, especially if the low time per cycle is much longer than the high time per cycle. If the low time per cycle is exactly equal to the high time per cycle, the signal is called a *square wave*.

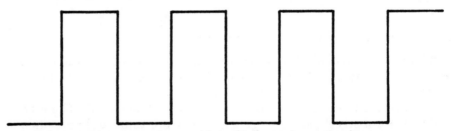

Fig. 1-6 *The output of an astable multivibrator is a rectangle wave.*

Because the output of an astable multivibrator is a periodic ac waveform, this type of circuit is often called an *oscillator*, a *signal generator*, a *pulse generator*, or a *rectangle-wave generator*.

The basic 555 astable multivibrator circuit appears in Fig. 1-7. Compare this circuit with the basic 555 monostable multivibrator circuit shown back in Fig. 1-4. Note that there is no external input connection in this circuit.

Once again, the basic circuitry is quite simple. Aside from the 555 timer IC itself, only four external components are required in this circuit: two resistors and two capacitors.

Capacitor C1 and resistors R1 and R2 control the timing period of the circuit. I discuss these components in some detail shortly.

Capacitor C2 is a simple bypass capacitor for the unused voltage-control input (pin #5). This bypass capacitor is not needed in all applications, but in some cases, if it is not used, the timer could exhibit some stability problems. I'd strongly advise always using the bypass capacitor in any 555 timer circuit whenever the voltage control input is

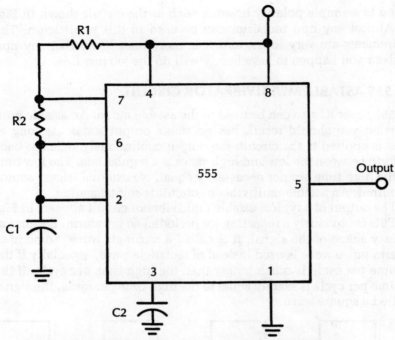

Fig. 1-7 *This is the basic 555 astable multivibrator circuit.*

not being used. It could save you some frustration when you run across a circuit that decides to act up. The bypass capacitor is cheap insurance.

A typical value for the bypass capacitor (C2) is 0.01 μF. The exact value is not at all critical. Changing the capacitor value will not noticeably affect circuit operation.

In some advanced applications, an external signal source is fed into the voltage control input (pin #5) to provide external control over the circuit's timing periods. Of course, if the voltage control input is being used, the bypass capacitor (C2) should be omitted from the circuitry.

The low time and the high time overlap in this circuit, but must be calculated separately. The high time calculation uses timing capacitor C1 and both timing resistors (R1 and R2). The formula for the low time, on the other hand uses only one of the timing resistors (R2), and the timing capacitor (C1).

The high time equation is:

$$T_h = 0.693C_1 (R_1 + R_2)$$

Don't worry about the derivation of the 0.693. It is a constant, defined by the internal circuitry of the 555 timer IC itself.

The formula for calculating the low time is similar, except the resistor R1 is omitted:

$$T_l = 0.693C_1R_2$$

Note that because the high time uses both resistances (R_1 and R_2) and the low time uses only one (R_2), the high time must always be longer than the low time. A true square wave (low time exactly equal to high time) is not possible with the basic 555 astable multivibrator circuit.

The total cycle time for this circuit is simply the sum of the high time and the low time. (The transistion times between the two states are extremely short and almost always negligible. They normally are ignored in the circuit design calculations.) The transistion time is:

$$T_t = T_h + T_1$$
$$= 0.693C_1 (R_1 + R_2) + 0.693C_1R_2$$
$$= 0.693C_1(R_1 + 2R_2)$$

Let's try out these formulas in a couple of typical examples. First, assume you are working with a 555 astable multivibrator circuit with the following component values:

$$R_1 = 22 \text{ k}\Omega$$
$$R_2 = 33 \text{ k}\Omega$$
$$C_1 = 0.1 \text{ } \mu\text{F}$$

Using these timing component values, the high time works out to:

$$T_h = 0.693 \times 0.0000001 \times (22,000 + 33,000)$$
$$= 0.693 \times 0.0000001 \times 55,000$$
$$= 0.0038115 \text{ second}$$
$$= 3,811.5 \text{ } \mu\text{S}$$

The low time is determined solely by capacitor C1 and resistor R2:

$$T_1 = 0.693 \times 0.0000001 \times 33,000$$
$$= 0.0022869 \text{ second}$$
$$= 2,286.9 \text{ } \mu\text{S}$$

The total cycle time is simply equal to the sum of the high time and the low time:

$$T_t = 0.0038115 + 0.0022869$$
$$= 0.0060984 \text{ second}$$
$$= 6098.4 \text{ } \mu\text{S}$$

For the second example, try using the following component values:

$$R_1 = 470 \text{ k}\Omega$$
$$R_2 = 100 \text{ k}\Omega$$
$$C_1 = 22 \text{ } \mu\text{F}$$

In this case, the high time works out to:

$$T_h = 0.693 \times 0.000022 \times (470,000 + 100,000)$$
$$= 0.693 \times 0.000022 \times 570,000$$
$$= 8.69 \text{ seconds}$$

The low time in this example is equal to:

$$T_1 = 0.693 \times 0.000022 \times 100,000$$
$$= 1.52 \text{ seconds}$$

This gives this sample circuit a total cycle time of:

$$T_t = 8.69 + 1.52$$
$$= 10.21 \text{ seconds}$$

Increasing the value(s) of any or all of the timing components (C1, R1, and R2) increases the time period(s) of the circuit. Remember, however, that resistor R1 controls only the high time. Changing the value of resistor R1 does not affect the low time.

The ratio of the high time to the total cycle time is known as the *duty cycle* of the rectangle wave. The duty cycle influences the harmonic content of the generated waveform, which can be significant in some applications. In the basic 555 astable multivibrator circuit, the duty cycle is defined by the relative values of the two timing resistors (R1 and R2):

$$R_2 : (R_1 + 2R_2)$$

When working with ac waveforms, such as the rectangle wave, it is generally more convenient to speak of frequency instead of cycle time. The conversion is easy enough, since frequency is simply the reciprocal of the total cycle time:

$$F = \frac{1}{T_t}$$
$$= \frac{1}{0.693 C_1 (R_1 + 2R_2)}$$

Frequency in Hertz (Hz) is a measurement of how many complete cycles occur per second. Let's take a moment to convert the results of our two sample problems into terms of frequency.

In the first example, the total cycle time was 0.0060984. If you take the reciprocal of this cycle time, you obtain a frequency of:

$$F = \frac{1}{0.0060984}$$
$$= 164 \text{ Hz}$$

In the second example, you had a total cycle time of 10.21 seconds. Converting this to frequency, you get a value of:

$$F = \frac{1}{10.21}$$
$$= 0.098 \text{ Hz}$$

Note that as the cycle time increases, the frequency decreases, and vice versa. Changing either the low time or the high time (or both) will alter the output frequency in this circuit.

The frequency of the output from a 555 astable multivibrator circuit can be calculated directly, without directly bothering with the timing periods at all.

For example, assume that the circuit has the following component values:

$$R_1 = 10 \text{ k}\Omega$$
$$R_2 = 22 \text{ k}\mu$$
$$C_1 = 0.05 \text{ }\mu\text{F}$$

In this example, the output frequency works out to an approximate value of:

$$
\begin{aligned}
F &= \frac{1}{0.693 C_1 \ (R_1 \ + \ 2R_2)} \\
&= \frac{1}{0.693 \ \times \ 0.00000005 \ \times \ (10{,}000 \ + \ 2 \ \times \ 22{,}000)} \\
&= \frac{1}{0.693 \ \times \ 0.00000005 \ \times \ (10{,}000 \ + \ 44{,}000)} \\
&= \frac{1}{0.693 \ \times \ 0.00000005 \ \times \ 54{,}000} \\
&= \frac{1}{0.0018711} \\
&= 534 \text{ Hz}
\end{aligned}
$$

Increasing the values of the timing components decreases the signal frequency at the circuit's output.

THE 556 DUAL-TIMER IC

So far in this chapter, I have spent quite a bit of time discussing the 555 timer IC. The primary focus in this book, however, is the 556 dual-timer IC. The time spent exploring the 555 certainly wasn't wasted by any means. The 556 is the exact electronic equivalent of two 555 timers in a single package.

The 556 dual-timer IC is usually contained within a 14-pin DIP housing, as illustrated in Fig. 1-8. Only two pins are used in common by both on-chip timer sections. These are the power-supply connections. Pin #14 is used for the positive supply voltage (V+), and pin #7 is the IC's ground connection.

A pair of separate 555 timer ICs can be used in place of a 556 dual-timer IC in any circuit. In virtually all circuits with two 555 timer ICs, a

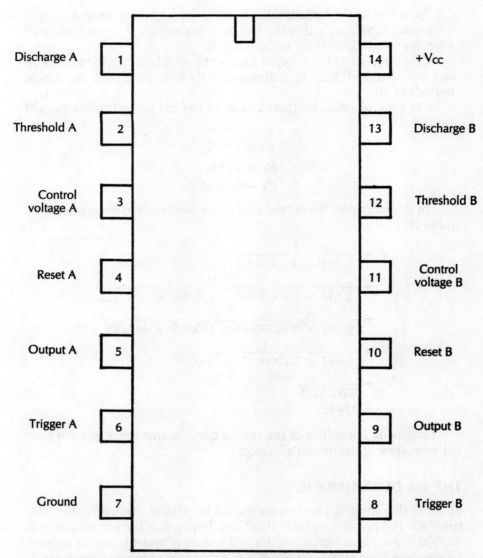

Discharge A — 1

Threshold A — 2

Control voltage A — 3

Reset A — 4

Output A — 5

Trigger A — 6

Ground — 7

+Vcc — 14

Discharge B — 13

Threshold B — 12

Control voltage B — 11

Reset B — 10

Output B — 9

Trigger B — 8

Fig. 1-8 *The 556 contains two 555-type timers in a single 14-pin package.*

556 dual-timer IC can be substituted. The only exception would be in a tiny handful of very exotic applications in which the two timer sections must use different supply voltages for some reason, or where the circuit grounds must be isolated from one another. Most electronics hobbyists will never encounter such a situation, so for all intents and purposes you can consider a 556 dual-timer IC as a direct and exact substitute for two separate 555 timer ICs. Aside from the power-supply connections, there is no need for any electrical connection or interaction between the two timer stages.

When substituting a 556 for two 555s (or vice versa), it is essential to match up the pin numbers correctly. The two chips are compared in Table 1-1.

Note that only pin #7 (ground) and pin #14 (V +) are used in common by both timer sections of the 556. Otherwise, the two timer sections in this chip are completely independent.

Table 1-1
Pin numbers and functions
for the 555 and 556 timers.

555 Timer	556 Timer A	556 Timer B	Function
1	7	7	Ground
2	6	8	Trigger
3	5	9	Output
4	4	10	Reset
5	3	11	Control voltage
6	2	12	Threshold
7	1	13	Discharge
8	14	14	V + (supply voltage)

The specifications for the 556 dual-timer IC are identical to those for the 555 timer IC. The supply voltage can range from + 4.5 V up to + 16 V, with + 5 V to + 15 V being the recommended limits for most applications.

The timing period is virtually independent from the supply voltage used to power the circuit. The timing period will fluctuate in response to a change in the circuit's supply voltage at a typical rate of 0.1% per volt. Component tolerances will account for much greater error in the vast majority of practical applications.

The 556, like the 555, is fully compatible with TTL and CMOS digital circuits, provided appropriate supply voltages are used.

THE 558 QUAD TIMER

Another close relative of the 555 and the 556 is the 558 quad-timer IC. This chip has four independent timer sections in a single 16-pin package. The pinout diagram for the 558 quad-timer IC appears in Fig. 1-9.

To reduce the number of required pins on this chip, some of the timer functions are not brought out to separate terminals. Each timer section has just three dedicated pins (ignoring the power supply, reset and control voltage pins that are in common to the IC as a whole):

- Output
- Timing
- Trigger

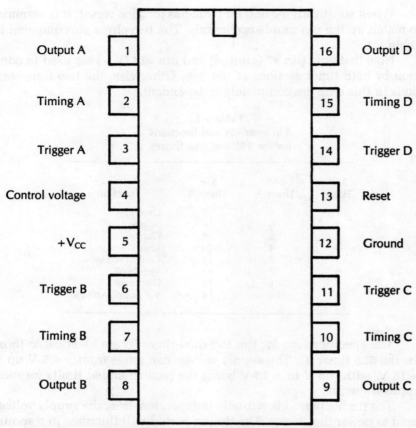

Output A	1		16	Output D
Timing A	2		15	Timing D
Trigger A	3		14	Trigger D
Control voltage	4		13	Reset
+V$_{CC}$	5		12	Ground
Trigger B	6		11	Trigger C
Timing B	7		10	Timing C
Output B	8		9	Output C

Fig. 1-9 *The 558 quad timer has four timer sections on a single chip.*

The "timing" pins on the 558 are somewhat equivalent to a combination of the 555 and 556 threshold and discharge pins, internally shorted together. These functions cannot be separated with the 558 timer. In addition, the reset function is not available.

Because of these limitations, the 558 quad-timer IC is not suitable for all applications involving 555 timer ICs or 556 dual-timer ICs. The 558 quad-timer IC is intended primarily for monostable multivibrator applications. The basic astable multivibrator circuit discussed earlier in this chapter is not possible with the 558.

You will not be using the 558 quad-timer IC for the projects in this book, but you should have at least a passing familiarity with this device.

THE 7555 CMOS TIMER

Another variation on the basic 555 timer IC you might be interested in is the 7555. This is a CMOS, rather than bipolar, device. In many circuits, the 555 can be replaced directly by the 7555. These two chips are pin-for-pin compatible.

Once again, I mention the 7555 CMOS timer IC here only for the sake of completeness. This chip will not be used in the projects described in the following chapters.

❖ 2
Timer projects

IN THIS FIRST CHAPTER OF PROJECTS, YOU WILL BE USING THE 556 DUAL-TIMER IC in a number of direct timing applications. Of course, this suggests that the timers will be used primarily in the monostable mode. Using multiple timer stages permits more complex timing cycles, and longer timing periods.

PROJECT 1: EXTENDED-RANGE TWO-STAGE TIMER

A two-stage monostable multivibrator circuit using the 556 dual-timer IC appears in Fig. 2-1. The output of the first timer stage triggers the next stage. Remember, a 555-type timer is triggered by a high-to-low transistion. This means the second timer will be triggered after the first stage times out. The time from the trigger to the end of the output pulse is the sum of the two timing periods:

$$T_t = T_1 + T_2$$

Typical input and output signals for this circuit appear in Fig. 2-2.

The operation of this two-stage circuit is easier to understand if you break up the 556 into two separate 555 timers, as shown in Fig. 2-3. This circuit is functionally identical to the circuit of Fig. 2-1. A typical parts list for this project appears in Table 2-1. The timing period for the first timer stage (T1) is controlled by the values of resistor R1 and capacitor C1, according to the basic 555 monostable multivibrator timing formula:

$$T_1 = 1.1R_1C_1$$

Similarly, the timing period of the second stage (T_2) is set by the values of resistor R2 and capacitor C3 using the same formula:

$$T_2 = 1.1R_2C_3$$

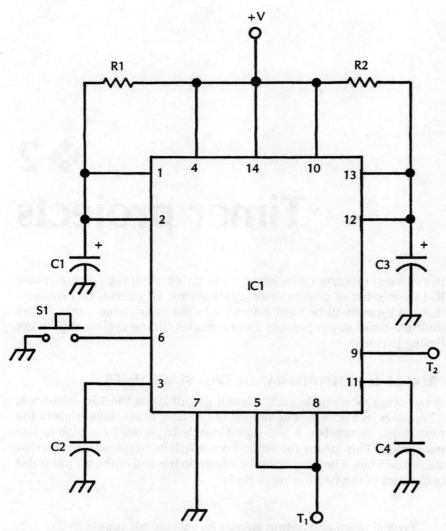

Fig. 2-1 *Project 1: Extended-range two-stage timer.*

The total delay time (T_t) set up by this circuit is simply the sum of the timing periods for the two individual stages:

$$T_t = T_1 + T_2$$
$$= 1.1R_1C_1 + 1.1R_2C_3$$
$$= 1.1 (R_1C_1 + R_2C_3)$$

To give you a better idea of how this circuit operates, we will solve for the timing periods using the suggested component values given in the parts list. You probably will want to experiment with alternate component values for the timing components—resistors R1 and R2 and

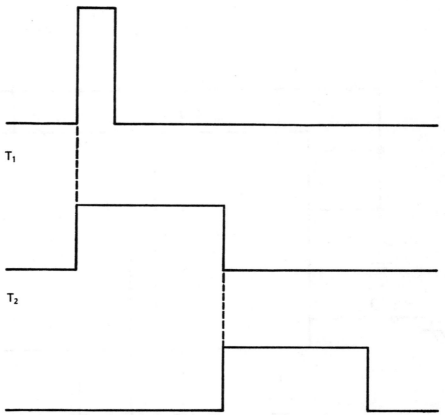

Fig. 2-2 *These are some typical input and output signals for the circuit of Fig. 2-1.*

capacitors C1 and C3. You might want to consider using potentiometers for the timing resistors to permit manual control over the timing periods in the circuit.

The parts list for this project suggests the following values for the circuit's timing components:

$$R_1 = 820 \text{ k}\Omega$$
$$R_2 = 680 \text{ k}\Omega$$
$$C_1 = 33 \text{ } \mu\text{F}$$
$$C_3 = 100 \text{ } \mu\text{F}$$

It is easy enough to solve the timing periods for each timer stage by plugging these component values into the standard equation. For the first timer stage (T_1), the timing period equals:

$$
\begin{aligned}
T_1 &= 1.1R_1C_1 \\
&= 1.1 \times 820,000 \times 0.000033 \\
&= 29.77 \text{ seconds}
\end{aligned}
$$

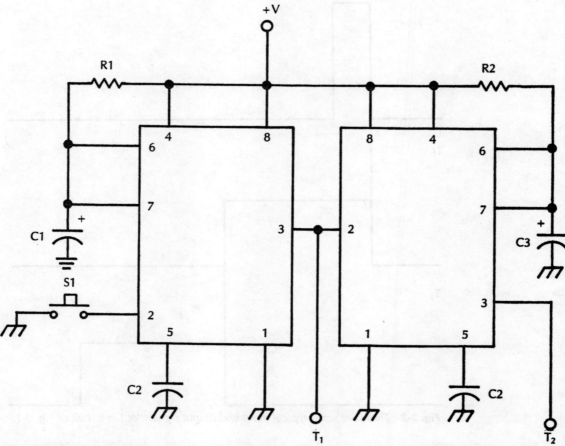

Fig. 2-3 *The circuit of Fig. 2-1 can be redrawn with two separate 555 timers instead of the 556 dual-timer.*

Table 2-1   Parts List for the Extended-Range Two-Stage Timer Project of Fig. 2-1.

IC1	556 dual-timer
C1	33-μF, 35-V electrolytic capacitor
C2, C4	0.01-μF capacitor
C3	100-μF, 35-V electrolytic capacitor
R1	820-kΩ, 1/4-W, 5% resistor
R2	680-kΩ, 1/4-W, 5% resistor
S1	Normally open SPST push button

The final output pulse (from the second timer stage, pin #9) begins about 30 seconds after the initial trigger pulse is received by the circuit. The length of this output pulse (T_2) is determined by the second timer stage:

$$T_2 = 1.1R_2C_3$$
$$= 1.1 \times 680,000 \times 0.0001$$
$$= 74.8 \text{ seconds}$$

or about $1\frac{1}{4}$ minutes.

The total timing period of the circuit as a whole is simply the sum of the delay time (T_1) and the output pulse time (T_2):

$$T_t = T_1 + T_2$$
$$= 29.77 + 74.8$$
$$= 104.57 \text{ seconds}$$
$$= 1 \text{ minute, } 44.57 \text{ seconds}$$

This is within the range of a single timer stage, of course. (Refer back to chapter 1.) However, this two-stage circuit offers the advantage of permitting smaller-value timing components. Stability and accuracy can get to be a problem with very large component values. This is especially true of capacitors.

Of course, extremely large timing periods can be set up by using larger values for the timing components. For example, assume that you have built the project using the following component values:

$$R_1 = 1 \text{ M}\Omega$$
$$R_2 = 3.3 \text{ M}\Omega$$
$$C_1 = 1000 \text{ } \mu\text{F}$$
$$C_3 = 500 \text{ } \mu\text{F}$$

In this case, the timing period of the first timer stage (T_1) works out to:

$$T_1 = 1.1 \times 1,000,000 \times 0.001$$
$$= 1,100 \text{ seconds}$$
$$= 18 \text{ minutes, } 20 \text{ seconds}$$

The timing period for the second timer stage (T_2) in this example works out to:

$$T_2 = 1.1 \times 3,300,000 \times 0.0005$$
$$= 1815 \text{ seconds}$$
$$= 30 \text{ minutes, } 15 \text{ seconds}$$

The total cycle time for this circuit is therefore equal to:

$$T_t = T_1 + T_2$$
$$= 1,100 + 1,815$$
$$= 2,915 \text{ seconds}$$
$$= 48 \text{ minutes, } 35 \text{ seconds}$$

In some applications, you might want to tap off the output pulse from the first timer stage, which is available at pin #5.

Capacitors C2 and C4 are simply stabilizing bypass capacitors, because the voltage-control inputs to the timers (pins #3 and #11) are not used in this application. In some case, they can be omitted, but they provide cheap insurance against possibly frustrating stability problems in some cases, particularly when very long timing periods are being used. Personally, I feel it is a good idea to always use the stabilizing bypass capacitors in every timer circuit, unless there is a specific reason not to.

The exact value of the bypass capacitors is not at all crucial. There is no point in experimenting with alternate values for capacitors C2 and C4 because changing these component values will not noticeably affect the circuit's operation in any way. A good general value for the bypass capacitors is 0.01 μF. You can substitute almost anything from 0.005 μF up to about 0.5 μF if that happens to be more convenient. Just use whatever capacitor in this range you happen to have handy. Of course, if you modify this circuit to use external voltage control of the timing periods, the bypass capacitors (C2 and C4) should be omitted from the circuit.

PROJECT 2: CONTINUOUS-OUTPUT-PULSE EXTENDED-RANGE TIMER

In the last project, the output pulse begins after a specific delay time (T_1). In some applications, you might need an extended-range output pulse that is continuous from the original trigger pulse up to the time the second stage times out.

In Fig. 2-4, the two-stage timer circuit from Fig. 2-1 is modified for a continuous output pulse. Figure 2-5 compares typical signals for these two circuits.

The key difference in this circuit is the addition of IC2, which is a pair of CMOS NOR gates. Naturally, this means that the supply voltage used for the project should be suitable for CMOS devices.

In this circuit, the second NOR gate is wired as an inverter, so the combination acts like an OR gate. The output of an OR gate is high if, and only if, input *A* is high or input *B* is high. If both inputs are low, the output will be low. This can be summarized in a simple truth table:

Inputs		Output
A	B	
L	L	L
L	H	H
H	L	H
H	H	H

where L indicates a low signal, and H represents a high signal. Note that this truth table covers all possible input combinations. The output will

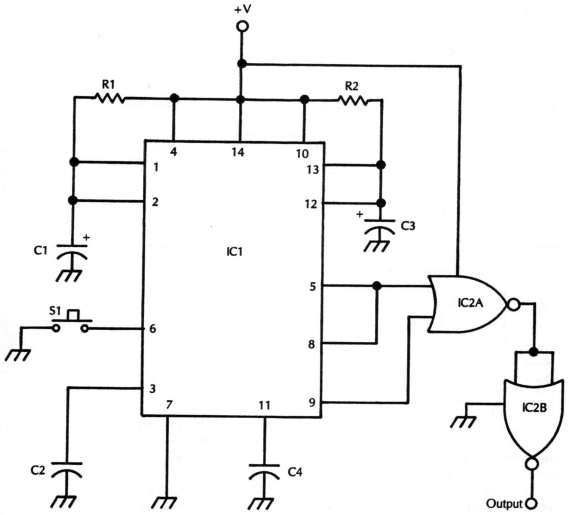

Fig. 2-4 *Project 2: Continuous-output-pulse extended-range timer.*

be high if both inputs are high, but in this particular circuit, that will never happen.

Normally, the output of both timer stages is low, so the output of the OR gate also is low. When the circuit is triggered, the output of timer stage A (T_1) goes high, bringing the circuit output (from the OR gate) high.

When the first timer stage times out, its output goes low, but at the same time, the second timer stage (T_2) is triggered, bringing its output high. The OR gate's output remains high.

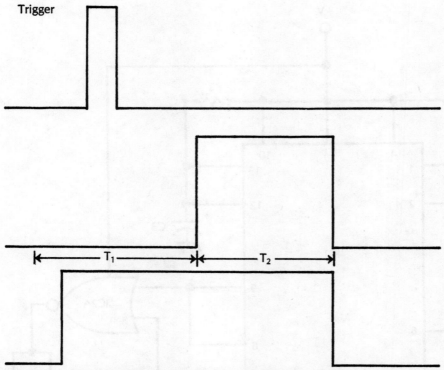

Trigger

T_1 T_2

Fig. 2-5 *This graph compares typical output signals for the circuits of Figs. 2-1 and 2-4.*

When the second timer stage times out, its output goes low, and the circuit output (from the OR gate) returns to its normal low state until the timer circuits receive another trigger pulse at the input. In all other respects this project is exactly the same as the preceding project.

A suitable parts list for this project is given in Table 2-2. I encourage you to experiment with alternate component values for the timing

Table 2-2 Parts List for the Continuous-Output-Pulse Extended-Range Timer Project of Fig. 2-4.

IC1	556 dual-timer
IC2	CD4001 quad NOR gate
C1	33-µF, 35-V electrolytic capacitor
C2, C4	0.01-µF capacitor
C3	100-µF, 35-V electrolytic capacitor
C5	0.1-µF capacitor
R1	820-kΩ, ¼-W, 5% resistor
R2	680-kΩ, ¼-W, 5% resistor
S1	Normally open SPST push button

components, resistors R1 and R2, and capacitors C1 and C3. Capacitors C2, C4, and C5 are simply stabilizing bypass capacitors, and there is no point in experimenting with alternate values for these components.

PROJECT 3: EXTENDED-RANGE FOUR-STAGE TIMER

Any number of timer stages can be cascaded in series to create extended timing periods. If you use two 556 dual-timer ICs, you can have up to four timer stages, as shown in Fig. 2-6. Each successive timer stage triggers the next timer along the line, with the final (fourth) stage providing the circuit's output. The first three stages set the delay period after the trigger pulse before the output pulse begins. The timing components in the last stage set the width (or length) of the circuit's output pulse.

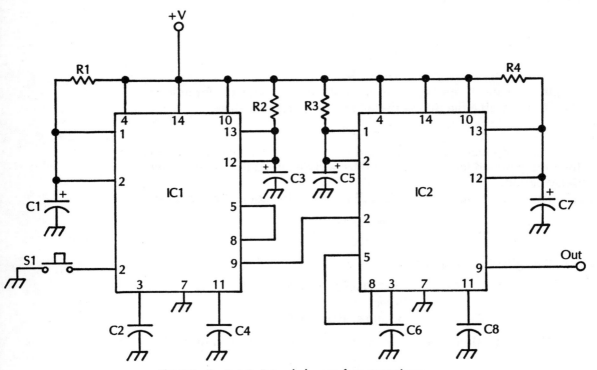

Fig. 2-6 Project 3: Extended-range four-stage timer.

A suitable parts list for this project is given in Table 2-3. By all means, experiment with alternate component values.

Capacitors C2, C4, C6, and C8 are stabilizing bypass capacitors for the unused voltage-control inputs. The values of these bypass capacitors do not affect the operation of the circuit, so don't bother experimenting with alternate values for these four capacitors.

**Table 2-3 Parts List for the
Extended-Range Four-Stage Timer Project of Fig. 2-6.**

IC1, IC2	556 dual-timer
C1, C3, C7	500-μF, 35-V electrolytic capacitor
C2, C4, C6, C8	0.01-μF capacitor
C5	250-μF, 35-V electrolytic capacitor
R1	2.2-MΩ, 1/4-W, 5% resistor
R2	10-MΩ, 1/4-W, 5% resistor
R3, R4	3.3-MΩ, 1/4-W, 5% resistor
S1	Normally open SPST pushbutton switch

Each timer stage has its own independent timing resistor and timing capacitor:

$$T_1: R1, C1$$
$$T_2: R2, C3$$
$$T_3: R3, C5$$
$$T_4: R4, C7$$

In each stage, the basic 555 monostable multivibrator formula is used to determine the timing period for that particular stage:

$$T = 1.1RC$$

The component values suggested in the parts list are fairly large, so the timing period for each stage will be fairly long, adding up to a long delay period.

The first timer stage uses the following timing component values:

$$R_1 = 2.2 \text{ M}\Omega$$
$$C_1 = 500 \text{ }\mu\text{F}$$

This gives us a first stage timing period of:

$$T_1 = 1.1 \times 2,200,000 \times 0.0005$$
$$= 1210 \text{ seconds}$$
$$= 20 \text{ minutes, 10 seconds}$$

The second timer stage uses the following component values:

$$R_2 = 10 \text{ M}\Omega$$
$$C_3 = 500 \text{ }\mu\text{F}$$

If you use these components, the timing period for this stage works out to:

$$T_2 = 1.1 \times 10,000,000 \times 0.0005$$
$$= 5500 \text{ seconds}$$
$$= 91 \text{ minutes, 40 seconds}$$
$$= 1 \text{ hour, 31 minutes, 40 seconds}$$

In the third stage, the suggested values for the timing components are:

$$R_3 = 3.3 \text{ M}\Omega$$
$$C_5 = 250 \ \mu\text{F}$$

As a result, the timing period for the third timer stage works out to:

$$T_3 = 1.1 \times 3,300,000 \times 0.00025$$
$$= 907.5 \text{ seconds}$$
$$= 15 \text{ minutes, 7.5 seconds}$$

In the fourth and final timer stage, the following parts values are suggested for the timing components:

$$R_4 = 3.3 \text{ M}\Omega$$
$$C_7 = 500 \ \mu\text{F}$$

This gives you an output pulse that last for a period of:

$$T_4 = 1.1 \times 3,300,000 \times 0.0005$$
$$= 1815 \text{ seconds}$$
$$= 30 \text{ minutes, 15 seconds}$$

After a trigger pulse is received at the input of this circuit, there will be a delay period before the output pulse begins. This delay time is equal to the sum of the timing periods of the first three timing stages:

$$T_d = T_1 + T_2 + T_3$$
$$= 1,210 + 5,500 + 907.5$$
$$= 7,617.5 \text{ seconds}$$
$$= 126 \text{ minutes, 57.5 seconds}$$
$$= 2 \text{ hours, 6 minutes, 57.5 seconds}$$

The length of the actual output pulse is controlled entirely by the fourth timer stage, and therefore is equal to T_4, or 1815 seconds in this case.

The circuit's total cycle time is equal to the sum of the delay time (T_d) plus the output pulse time (T_4):

$$T_t = T_d + T_4$$
$$= 7,617.5 + 1,815$$
$$= 9,432.5 \text{ seconds}$$
$$= 157 \text{ minutes, 12.5 seconds}$$
$$= 2 \text{ hours, 37 minutes, 12.5 seconds}$$

Of course, changing the value of any or all of the timing components in this circuit will alter the overall timing.

PROJECT 4: FOUR-STAGE-SEQUENTIAL TIMER

The circuit shown in Fig. 2-7 is very similar to the one shown previously in Fig. 2-6. The difference here is that you are tapping off the intermediate outputs to create a sequential timer.

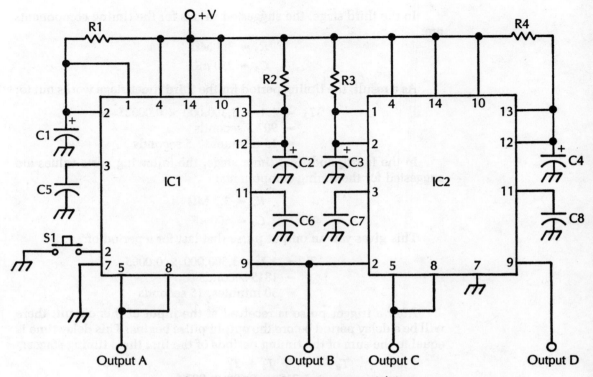

Fig. 2-7 *Project 4: Four-stage-sequential timer.*

Figure 2-8 illustrates the action of this circuit with typical input and output signals. When the circuit is triggered, output T_1 is activated immediately. When this timer stage times out, the second output (T_2) is brought high. After the timing cycle of the second timer stage, output T_2 goes low, and output T_3 goes high. When this timer stage completes its cycle, the fourth and final output (T_4) is activated for the duration of the fourth timer stage's timing period. Note that only one of the four outputs is high at any given instant.

This circuit can be used to control sequentially almost any electrically controllable device. Assuming a suitable supply voltage is used for the circuit, the outputs can drive digital as well as linear circuitry. In fact, there is no reason why the two can't be combined together. For example, outputs T_1 and T_4 could drive linear circuits, while outputs T_2 and T_3 could control digital circuits. The possible applications for this project are limited only by your imagination.

A suitable parts list for this project appears in Table 2-4. You can experiment with alternate component values.

Capacitors C2, C4, C6, and C8 are stabilizing bypass capacitors for the unused voltage-control inputs. The values of these bypass capacitors do not affect the operation of the circuit, so don't bother experimenting with alternate values for these four capacitors.

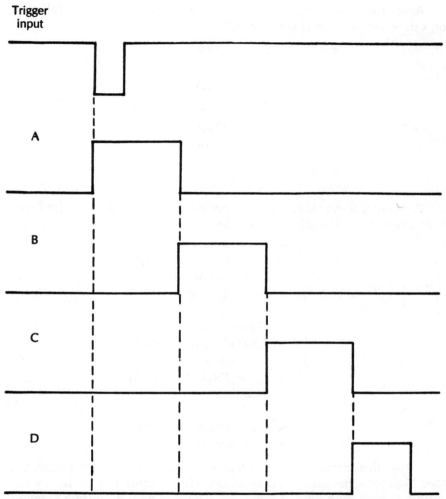

Fig. 2-8 *These are some typical input and output signals for the circuit of Fig. 2-7.*

**Table 2-4   Parts List for the
Four-Stage-Sequential Timer Project of Fig. 2-7.**

IC1, IC2	556 dual-timer
C1, C3	100-μF, 35-V electrolytic capacitor
C5, C6, C7, C8	0.01-μF capacitor
C2	250-μF, 35-V electrolytic capacitor
C4	50-μF, 35-V electrolytic capacitor
R1, R4	470-kΩ, 1/4-W, 5% resistor
R2	1-MΩ, 1/4-W, 5% resistor
R3	220-kΩ, 1/4-W, 5% resistor
S1	Normally open SPST pushbutton switch

According to this suggested parts list, you will be using the following values for the timing components:

$$R_1 = 470 \text{ k}\Omega$$
$$R_2 = 1 \text{ M}\Omega$$
$$R_3 = 220 \text{ k}\Omega$$
$$R_4 = 470 \text{ k}\Omega$$
$$C_1 = 100 \text{ } \mu\text{F}$$
$$C_2 = 250 \text{ } \mu\text{F}$$
$$C_3 = 100 \text{ } \mu\text{F}$$
$$C_4 = 50 \text{ } \mu\text{F}$$

Assuming these component values are used in the circuit, the four timing periods will work out to the following values:

$$
\begin{aligned}
T_1 &= 1.1 \times R_1 \times C_1 \\
&= 1.1 \times 470{,}000 \times 0.0001 \\
&= 51.7 \text{ seconds}
\end{aligned}
$$

$$
\begin{aligned}
T_2 &= 1.1 \times R_2 \times C_3 \\
&= 1.1 \times 1{,}000{,}000 \times 0.00025 \\
&= 275 \text{ seconds} \\
&= 4 \text{ minutes, 35 seconds}
\end{aligned}
$$

$$
\begin{aligned}
T_3 &= 1.1 \times R_3 \times C_5 \\
&= 1.1 \times 220{,}000 \times 0.0001 \\
&= 24.2 \text{ seconds}
\end{aligned}
$$

$$
\begin{aligned}
T_4 &= 1.1 \times R_4 \times C_7 \\
&= 1.1 \times 470{,}000 \times 0.00005 \\
&= 25.85 \text{ seconds}
\end{aligned}
$$

When this circuit receives a trigger pulse, output T_1 immediately goes high for a period of 51.7 seconds. Then output T_1 goes low, and output T_2 goes high for 275 seconds. After this period, output T_2 goes low, and output T_3 goes high. After 24.2 seconds, output T_3 goes low again, and output T_4 goes high for a period of 25.85 seconds. Then output T_4 goes low, and all four outputs remain low until the next incoming trigger pulse is detected by the circuit.

Once the first timer stage (T_1) has timed out, the circuit can be retriggered. This results in more than one of the outputs being high simultaneously.

Assuming there is just a single trigger pulse, the circuit's total cycle time is just the sum of the four individual timing periods:

$$T_t = T_1 + T_2 + T_3 + T_4$$

For our example, this works out to:

$$T_t = 51.7 + 275 + 24.2 + 25.85$$
$$= 376.75 \text{ seconds}$$
$$= 6 \text{ minutes, } 16.75 \text{ seconds}$$

PROJECT 5: CYCLIC FOUR-STAGE-SEQUENTIAL TIMER

The circuit shown in Fig. 2-9 is almost identical to the one shown in Fig. 2-7, with the exception of one important modification. The final output (T_4) is fed back into the trigger input. When the fourth timer stage times out, it will automatically retrigger the first timer stage, restarting the entire timing-cycle sequence. Once this circuit has received one trigger pulse, the sequential output pattern continues indefinitely, unless the circuit's voltage supply is removed.

A typical parts list for this project appears in Table 2-5. As always, I encourage you to experiment with alternate component values.

**Table 2-5 Parts List for the
Cyclic Four-Stage-Sequential Timer Project of Fig. 2-9.**

IC1, IC2	556 dual-timer
C1, C3	500-μF, 35-V electrolytic capacitor
C2, C4, C6, C8	0.01-μF capacitor
C5, C7	250-μF, 35-V electrolytic capacitor
R1	470-kΩ, 1/4-W, 5% resistor
R2, R4	1-MΩ, 1/4-W, 5% resistor
R3	680-kΩ, 1/4-W, 5% resistor
R5	10-MΩ, 1/4-W, 5% resistor
S1	Normally open SPST pushbutton switch

PROJECT 6: SIMULTANEOUS DELAYED PULSES

In the extended-range timer projects presented so far in this chapter, all of the timer stages have been in series, operating one after another. In this project, you also will be using timers in parallel.

The schematic diagram for this project appears in Fig. 2-10, and Table 2-6 shows a typical parts list. Feel free to experiment with alternate values for the timing components in this circuit.

Because two 556 dual-timer ICs are used in this circuit, there are four timer stages. All four stages use their timers in the monostable mode.

The circuit has three outputs: *A*, *B*, and *C*. These outputs are taken from three timer stages wired in parallel. All three of these monostable timers are triggered in unison. This means their output pulses all begin

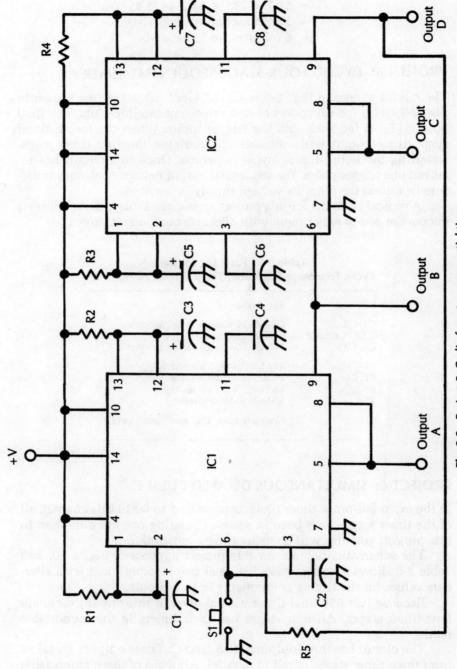

Fig. 2-9 *Project 5: Cyclic four-stage sequential timer.*

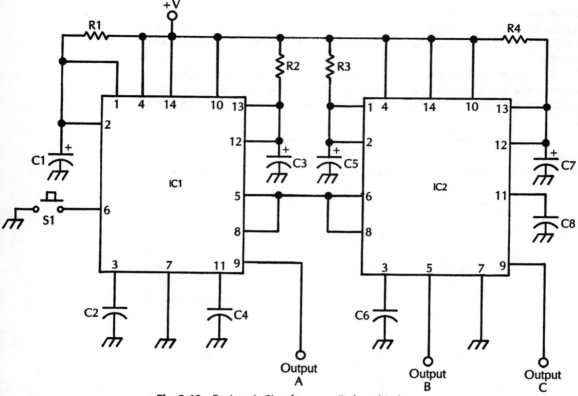

Fig. 2-10   *Project 6: Simultaneous Delayed Pulses.*

**Table 2-6   Parts List for the
Simultaneous-Delayed Pulses Project of Fig. 2-10.**

IC1, IC2	556 dual-timer
C1, C5	50-μF, 35-V electrolytic capacitor
C2, C4, C6, C8	0.01-μF capacitor
C3	25-μF, 35-V electrolytic capacitor
C7	10-μF, 35-V electrolytic capacitor
R1	100-kΩ, 1/4-W, 5% resistor
R2	220-kΩ, 1/4-W, 5% resistor
R3	470-kΩ, 1/4-W, 5% resistor
R4	390-kΩ, 1/4-W, 5% resistor
S1	Normally open SPST pushbutton switch

at the same time. The length of each output pulse, of course, is determined by the values of the timing resistor and capacitor in that particular timer stage. The paralleled timer stages do not interact with one another.

The trigger pulse for the three paralleled timers comes from the output of a fourth timer stage in series with the parallel combination. This is made clear by the block diagram for this circuit shown in Fig. 2-11.

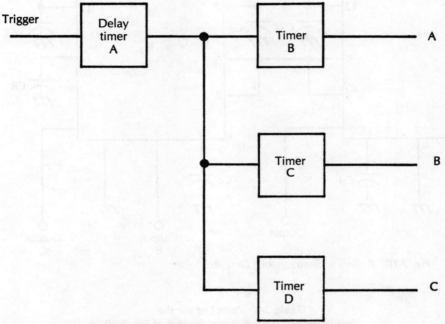

Fig. 2-11 *This is a block diagram for the circuit of Fig. 2-10.*

When the circuit receives a suitable trigger pulse, the output of the first (series) timer stage goes high for a period determined by resistor R1 and capacitor C1. When this timer stage times out, its output goes low. The high-to-low transistion simultaneously triggers the three remaining (parallel) timer stages. In other words, when the circuit is triggered, there is a specific delay, then all three outputs are simultaneously activated for varying lengths of time, depending on the values of the timing components in the individual timer stage. Figure 2-12 illustrates the operations of this circuit with typical input and output signals.

The first timer stage uses resistor R1 and capacitor C1 to set the delay time after the trigger pulse before the output pulses begin. The parts list suggests the following component values:

$$R_1 = 100 \text{ k}\Omega$$
$$C_1 = 50 \text{ }\mu\text{F}$$

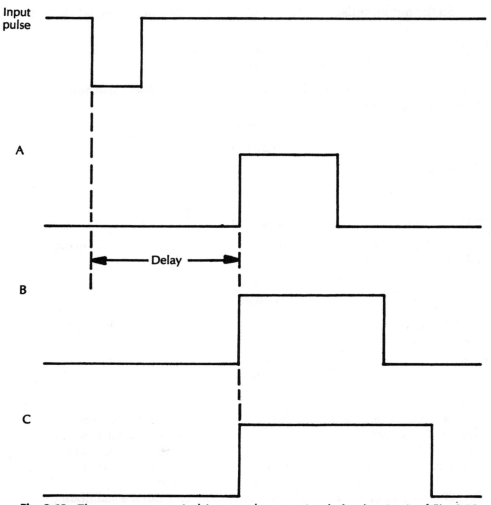

Fig. 2-12 *These are some typical input and output signals for the circuit of Fig. 2-10.*

This gives the circuit a delay time of:

$$T_d = 1.1R_1C_1$$
$$= 1.1 \times 100,000 \times 0.00005$$
$$= 5.5 \text{ seconds}$$

When a trigger pulse is received, nothing will happen for five and a half seconds. Then all three outputs (A, B, and C) all go high.

Timer A uses the following timing components:

$$R_2 = 220 \text{ k}\Omega$$
$$C_3 = 25 \text{ } \mu\text{F}$$

So the output pulse at output A should last for a period equal to:

$$T_a = 1.1R_2C_3$$
$$= 1.1 \times 220,000 \times 0.000025$$
$$= 6.05 \text{ seconds}$$

Meanwhile, timer stage B is using the following suggested values for its timing components:

$$R_3 = 470 \text{ k}\Omega$$
$$C_5 = 50 \text{ }\mu F$$

This results in a pulse at output B lasting:

$$T_b = 1.1R_3C_5$$
$$= 1.1 \times 470,000 \times 0.00005$$
$$= 25.85 \text{ seconds}$$

Finally, for the last timer stage (C), the parts list gives the following values for the timing components:

$$R_4 = 390 \text{ k}\Omega$$
$$C_7 = 10 \text{ }\mu F$$

Therefore, using these component values, C's output pulse length works out to:

$$T_c = 1.1R_4C_7$$
$$= 1.1 \times 390,000 \times 0.00001$$
$$= 4.29 \text{ seconds}$$

Of course, any or all of the timing component values can be changed for other timing periods. Increasing either the resistor value or the capacitor value increases the timing period for that particular stage. Of course, reducing the value of one (or both) of the timing components results in a shorter timing period for that particular stage.

The even-numbered capacitors (C2, C4, C6, and C8) are stabilizing bypass capacitors for the unused voltage-control inputs of the four timer stages. The exact value used for these bypass capacitors is not at all crucial and does not noticeably affect the operation of the circuit. As usual, there is little point in experimenting with alternate values for the bypass capacitors.

PROJECT 7: DUAL-ACTION TIMER

Another cascaded timer circuit using the 556 dual-timer IC appears in Fig. 2-13. There are two outputs from this circuit. Normally, both outputs are low. When the timer is triggered by pushing the normally open pushbutton or by an external trigger signal, output A immediately goes high for a period of time determined by the values of potentiometer R1,

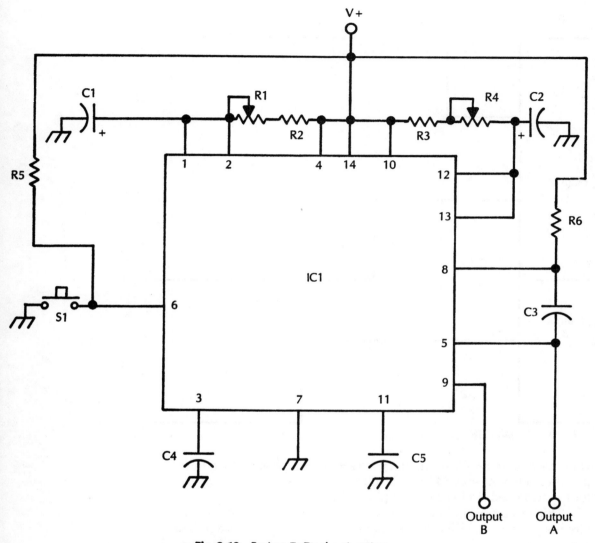

Fig. 2-13 *Project 7: Dual-action timer.*

resistor R2, and capacitor C1. When this timer stage completes its timing cycle, output *A* reverts to its normal low state, and output *B* goes high for a period determined by the values of resistor R3, potentiometer R4, and capacitor C2. After this timing period is over, output *B* goes back low too, and the circuit waits for the next incoming trigger pulse. A set of typical input and output signals for this circuit appears in Fig. 2-14.

Potentiometers R1 and R4 are included in the circuit to permit manual control over the two timing periods. If this feature is not required in

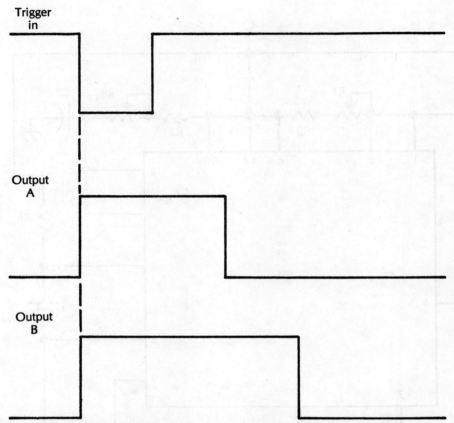

Fig. 2-14 *These are typical input and output signals for the circuit of Fig. 2-13.*

your particular application, it is a very simple matter to eliminate potentiometers R1 and R4 from the circuit and select appropriate values for the two fixed timing resistors (R2 and R3).

This circuit is similar to the other cascaded extended-range timer circuits presented in this chapter, but the coupling system is a little different in this case. The output of the first timer stage (pin #5) is coupled to the trigger input of the second timer stage through capacitor C3. The value of this coupling capacitor is not very important.

Capacitors C4 and C5 are simply the stabilizing bypass capacitors for the unused voltage-control inputs. The values of these capacitors are also relatively unimportant.

Resistors R5 and R6 are pull-up resistors to hold the trigger inputs of the two timer stages high, except when a negative-going trigger pulse forces the appropriate trigger pin low.

Table 2-7 shows a typical parts list for this project. As always, I encourage you to experiment with alternate component values, especially with capacitors C1 and C2 and resistors R2 and R3.

**Table 2-7   Parts List for the
Dual-Action Timer Project of Fig. 2-13.**

IC1	556 dual-timer
C1	100-μF, 35-V electrolytic capacitor
C2	250-μF, 35-V electrolytic capacitor
C3, C4, C5	0.01-μF capacitor
R1, R4	1-MΩ potentiometer
R2	220-kΩ, 1/4-W, 5% resistor
R3	330-kΩ, 1/4-W, 5% resistor
R5, R6	100-kΩ, 1/4-W, 5% resistor
S1	Normally open SPST pushbutton switch (optional—see text)

The first step is to work out the circuit's timing periods for the suggested component values from the parts list. Both timer stages in this circuit are monostable multivibrators, using the standard monostable timing equation:

$$T = 1.1RC$$

In this case, R is the series combination (sum) of the setting of the potentiometer (R1 or R4) and the fixed resistor (R2 or R3). For the sake of simplicity, we will assume each potentiometer is set at the exact midpoint of its range.

The first monostable multivibrator stage uses the following component values:

$$C = C_1 = 100\ \mu F$$
$$R_1 = 500\ k\Omega$$

(1-MΩ potentiometer)

$$R_2 = 220\ k\Omega$$
$$R = R_1 + R_2$$
$$= 500\ k\Omega + 220\ k\Omega$$
$$= 720\ k\Omega$$

This makes the first stage timing period equal to:

$$T = 1.1 \times 720{,}000 \times 0.0001$$
$$= 79.2\ \text{seconds}$$
$$= 1\ \text{minute, 19.2 seconds}$$

Similarly, the component values in the second monostable multivibrator stage are as follows:

$$C = C_2 = 250\ \mu F$$
$$R_3 = 330\ k\Omega$$
$$R_4 = 500\ k\Omega$$

(1-MΩ potentiometer)

$$R = R_3 + R_4$$
$$= 330 \text{ k}\Omega + 500 \text{ k}\Omega$$
$$= 830 \text{ k}\Omega$$

This makes the second stage timing period equal to:

$$T = 1.1 \times 830,000 \times 0.00025$$
$$= 228.25 \text{ seconds}$$
$$= 3 \text{ minutes, } 48.25 \text{ seconds}$$

Using these component values, when the circuit is first triggered, output *A* immediately goes high, while output *B* remains low for a period of approximately 1 minute, 20 seconds. Then output *A* goes low and output *B* goes high for a little under four minutes. After this timing period, both outputs are in their normal, low state until the next trigger pulse.

PROJECT 8: VERY EXTENDED TIME DELAY

By combining timer-based monostable multivibrator circuits with digital counter circuitry, very extended timing periods are possible. Figure 2-15 shows a circuit of this type. A suitable parts list for this project appears in Table 2-8.

Table 2-8 Parts List for the Very Extended-Time Delay Project of Fig. 2-15.

IC1	556 dual-timer
IC2	7490 decade counter
IC3	7400 quad NOR gate
S1	SP6T rotary switch
C1	100-μF, 35-V electrolytic capacitor
C2, C3, C5	0.01-μF capacitor
C4	50-μF, 35-V electrolytic capacitor
R1	1-MΩ, 1/4-W, 5% resistor
R2, R3	1-MΩ potentiometer
R4	10-kΩ, 1/4-W, 5% resistor

Because TTL gates are used in this circuit, the power supply should be a well-regulated +5 V. You could substitute comparable CMOS devices if you prefer.

The 7490 (IC2) is a decade counter, which divides the base timer period by 2, 5, or 10. The division factor is selected by rotary switch (S1). In the lowest position, the circuit is disabled effectively, because the slider of the switch isn't connected to anything. In the second position, the switch slider is shorted to pin #12 of IC2. This gives a time

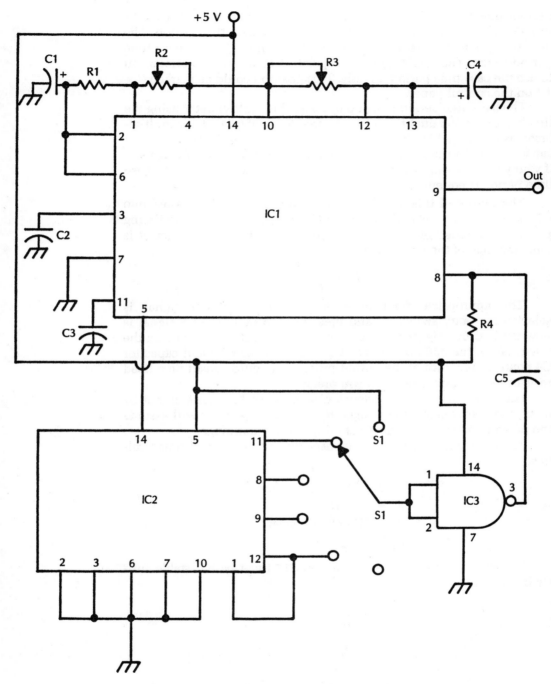

Fig. 2-15 Project 8: Very extended time delay.

period equal to twice the base time period. The next position uses IC2's pin #9 for a timing period equal to five times the base time period. The next two positions (pin #8 and pin #11) both multiply the base time period by ten. The final (uppermost) position of switch S1 permits you to use the base time period directly. This position could be marked "× 1" on the control panel.

The base time period is set up by an astable multivibrator using the first half of the 556 dual-timer IC. The frequency of this astable multivibrator is controlled by the values of resistor R1, potentiometer R2, and capacitor C1. You can replace potentiometer R2 by a fixed-value resistor if your particular application doesn't require manual control of the base time period (frequency).

The output of this astable multivibrator (pin #5—IC1) is fed into IC2 to be counted, or divided. By reducing the frequency, the timing period is extended effectively, because by definition the frequency is the reciprocal of the time period:

$$F = \frac{1}{T}$$

The appropriate frequency-reduced (time-extended) signal is selected by rotary switch S1 and then inverted by IC3. This signal is now fed into the trigger input of a monostable multivibrator using the other half of the 556 dual-timer (IC1). Potentiometer R3 and capacitor C4 control the width of the output pulse. You could substitute a fixed resistor for potentiometer R3 if you prefer.

Let's see how the time-extension process works in this circuit by using the component values suggested in the parts list. I will assume the potentiometers are at the exact midpoint of their range.

The astable multivibrator stage uses the following component values:

$$R_1 = 1 \text{ M}\Omega$$
$$R_2 = 500 \text{ k}\Omega$$
$$(1 - \text{M}\Omega \text{ potentiometer})$$
$$C_1 = 100 \text{ }\mu\text{F}$$

The standard frequency equation for a 555 timer-based astable multivibrator is used:

$$
\begin{aligned}
F &= \frac{1}{0.693 C_1 (R_2 + 2R_1)} \\
&= \frac{1}{0.693 \times 0.0001 \times (500,000 + 2 \times 1,000,000)} \\
&= \frac{1}{0.693 \times 0.0001 \times (500,000 + 2,000,000)} \\
&= \frac{1}{0.693 \times 0.0001 \times 2,500,000}
\end{aligned}
$$

$$= \frac{1}{275}$$
$$= 0.0036 \text{ Hz}$$

There is one pulse every 275 seconds (or about 4½ minutes).

Depending on the setting of rotary switch S1, you can select any of the following delay periods:

× 1	275 seconds
× 2	550 seconds
× 5	1,375 seconds
× 10	2,750 seconds

At the × 10 setting, there is one pulse about every 46 minutes.

The width of the output pulse is set by the monostable multivibrator stage, using the following components:

$$R_3 = 500 \text{ k}\Omega$$

(1-MΩ potentiometer)

$$C_4 = 50 \text{ } \mu\text{F}$$

This gives you an output pulse with a period equal to:

$$T = 1.1R_3C_4$$
$$= 1.1 \times 500,000 \times 0.00005$$
$$= 27.5 \text{ seconds}$$

Capacitors C2 and C3 are stabilizing bypass capacitors for the unused voltage-control inputs in the timers.

PROJECT 9: RAMP TIMER

Most timer circuits provide only simple on/off control. That is, the output is either low, or it is high. There are no intermediate states. (The transistion time between states is considered negligible.) This is true of all of the timer projects presented so far in this chapter.

In some specialized applications, however, it could be desirable to have the output voltage change gradually over time, going from a minimum (low) value smoothly up to a maximum (high) value in a specific, preset period of time. The timer circuit shown in Fig. 2-16 will do just this.

Unlike most of the projects in this book, this circuit uses just a single timer section. It can be built around half a 556 dual-timer IC. The open pin numbers given in the schematic diagram are for timer A. If you prefer to use timer B, use the pin numbers given in parentheses. The power-supply connections (pin #14—V + , and pin #7—ground) are the same for both of the 556's timer sections. The unused timer section can be used for additional circuitry in a larger system.

Because only a single timer section is used in this project, you can

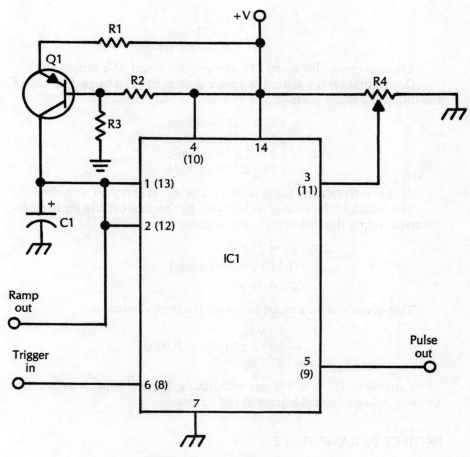

Fig. 2-16 *Project 9: Ramp timer.*

substitute a 555 timer IC for the 556 chip. Change the pin numbers as
listed below:

556	555
1	7
2	6
3	5
4	4
5	3
6	2
7	1
14	8

A suitable parts list for this unusual timer project appears in Table
2-9. You can experiment with alternate component values.

**Table 2-9   Parts List for the
Ramp-Timer Project of Fig. 2-16.**

IC1	556 dual-timer
Q1	pnp transistor (2N3906, or similar)
C1	50-μF, 35-V electrolytic capacitor
R1	100-kΩ, 1/4-W, 5% resistor
R2	4.7-kΩ, 1/4-W, 5% resistor
R3	10-kΩ, 1/4-W, 5% resistor
R4	10-kΩ potentiometer (see text)

The ramp output is tapped off from the timer's discharge (pin #1) and threshold (pin #2) terminals. In effect, this output is the voltage across the timing capacitor (C1). The ordinary pulse output is also simultaneously available from the timer's output pin (#5). The two outputs are always in synchrony with one another, beginning and ending at the same time. Figure 2-17 illustrates typical input and output signals for this ramp-timer circuit.

You are taking the ramp output off of timing capacitor (C1). Unfortunately, a capacitor normally charges in an exponential, rather than a linear fashion. This would result in a very curved ramp output, as shown in Fig. 2-18. This might not matter in some applications, but you want this circuit to put out a linear ramp.

A capacitor can be charged linearly through a constant-current source. In this circuit, the ordinary timing resistor has been replaced by transistor Q1. This transistor functions as a constant-current source.

The resistor (R1) in the emitter circuit of the transistor is the new timing resistor for the ramp timer circuit. Changing the value of this resistor will alter the time it takes the capacitor to charge, and thus, the circuit's timing period.

There is a price for this modification, however. The timing-period equation in this circuit is somewhat more complex than in most 555 monostable multivibrator circuits:

$$T = \frac{V_c C_1}{I_t}$$

In this equation, T is the circuit's timing period in seconds, and C_1 is the value of the timing capacitor in farads. V_c is the voltage fed to the timer's control-voltage input (pin #3). This voltage is set by the simple resistive voltage divider made up of potentiometer R4. Moving the potentiometer's slider changes the control voltage (V_c). This in turn affects the circuit's timing period. In an application not requiring manual control of the timing period, this potentiometer (R4) can be replaced

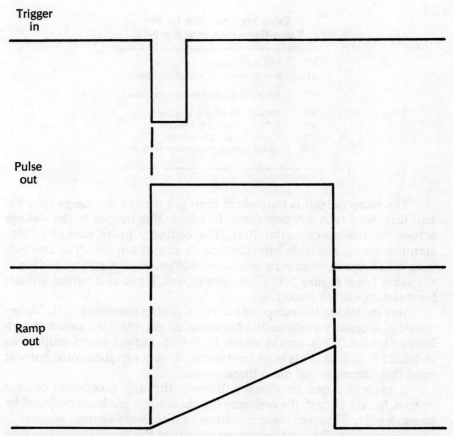

Fig. 2-17 *These are typical input and output signals for the circuit of Fig. 2-16.*

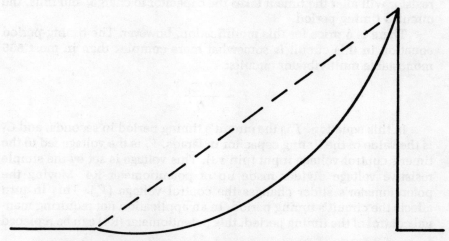

Fig. 2-18 *Nonlinear charging of the capacitor produces a curved ramp.*

by a pair of fixed resistors in series. The control voltage (pin #3) is tapped off at the common point between the two resistors.

The current output of transistor Q1 is determined by the value of resistor R1 and the circuit's supply voltage. Assuming a + 15-V supply voltage, the I_t current approximately equals:

$$I_t = \frac{4.2}{R_1}$$

This equation is not precisely correct, but it will be close enough for most applications. In critical applications, a trimpot can be used for resistor R1, permitting you to adjust the resistance precisely by monitoring the transistor's output with a milliammeter.

If you algebraically rearrange the timing equation and the transistor current equation, you get a somewhat simpler approximate formula for the circuit's timing period:

$$T = 0.24 V_c C_1 R_1$$

It is important to remember that this equation assumes a supply voltage of + 15 V for the circuit. This is the recommended supply voltage for this particular project. The circuit will work with lower supply voltages, but at a loss in accuracy and overall stability, and the current equation will have to be reworked.

Let's assume that the V_c potentiometer (R4) is set to the exact midpoint of its range. This would make V_c equal to one-half the circuit's supply voltage, or:

$$V_c = \frac{V+}{2}$$
$$= \frac{15}{2}$$
$$= 7.5 \text{ volts}$$

The same effect can be achieved by replacing the potentiometer with two identical resistors in series.

With this V_c setting being held constant, you can simplify the timing equation a little further:

$$
\begin{aligned}
T &= 0.24 V_c C_1 R_1 \\
&= 0.24 \times 7.5 \times C_1 R_1 \\
&= 1.8 C_1 R_1
\end{aligned}
$$

Using the suggested component values from the parts list, you now can solve for the timing period of the circuit:

$$
\begin{aligned}
C_1 &= 50 \ \mu F \\
R_1 &= 100 \ k\Omega \\
T &= 1.8 \times 0.00005 \times 100,000 \\
&\approx 9 \text{ seconds}
\end{aligned}
$$

To see how this circuit works, connect a flashlight bulb between the ramp output and ground. When the timer circuit is triggered, the bulb should light dimly, and gradually increase to full brightness, then abruptly cut off at the end of the timing cycle. The lamp might not glow for a second or so after the circuit has first been triggered. The voltage applied to lightbulb must exceed a specific base value before the filament will start to glow.

The ramp output also can be monitored with a voltmeter (especially when shorter timing periods are used), or with an oscilloscope. As always, you can experiment with alternate component values. Resistors R2 and R3 affect the gain of the transistor (Q1), and thus, its constant-current output. Almost any low-signal pnp transistor should work fairly well for Q1 in this circuit.

PROJECT 10: EXTREMELY LONG-RANGE TIMER

There are a great many ways to extend the range of a timer. For extremely long timing periods, try the circuit shown in Fig. 2-19. A suitable parts list for this project appears in Table 2-10.

Only half of the 556 timer IC is used in this project. The other half can be put to work in other circuitry in a larger system of your own design. If timer A is used, follow the open pin numbers in the schematic diagram. For timer B, use the pin numbers given in parentheses

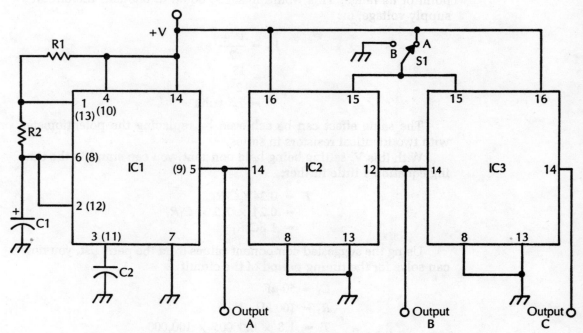

Fig. 2-19 *Project 10: Extremely long-range timer.*

Table 2-10
Parts List for the Extremely
Long-Range Timer Project of Fig. 2-19.

IC1	556 dual-timer
IC2, IC3	CD4017 CMOS decade counter
S1	SPDT switch
C1	100-µF, 35-V electrolytic capacitor
C2	0.01-µF capacitor
R1	820-kΩ, 1/4-W, 5% resistor
R2	3.9-kΩ, 1/4-W, 5% resistor

in the drawing. The power-supply connections (pin #14—V + , and pin #7—ground) are used by both of the 556's timer stages.

If you prefer, you could substitute a 555 single-timer chip for IC1 in this project. Correct the pin numbers, as explained back in chapter 1.

The supply voltage for this project should be suitable for use with CMOS digital gates, because IC2 and IC3 are CD4017 decade counters.

This circuit has three separate outputs, labeled *A*, *B*, and *C* in the schematic diagram. Output *A* is simply the direct output signal from the timer (IC1), which is wired as an astable multivibrator. The suggested parts list has the following component values:

$$C_1 = 100 \ \mu\text{F}$$
$$R_1 = 820 \ \text{k}\Omega$$
$$R_2 = 3.9 \ \text{k}\Omega$$

Using these particular component values, the circuit's base frequency works out to approximately:

$$
\begin{aligned}
F &= \frac{1}{0.693 \times 0.0001 \times (820{,}000 + 2 \times 3900)} \\
&= \frac{1}{0.693 \times 0.0001 \times (820{,}000 + 7800)} \\
&= \frac{1}{0.693 \times 0.0001 \times 827{,}800} \\
&= \frac{1}{57.4} \\
&= 0.017 \ \text{Hz}
\end{aligned}
$$

There is one output pulse approximately every 57 seconds (or a little less than once per minute). Of course, as with all the projects in this book, I encourage you to experiment with alternate component values for different timing periods.

This signal is also fed into the input of the first decade counter (IC2). This IC effectively divides its input frequency by a factor of ten.

That is, there is one output pulse for every ten input pulses. So, using the suggested component values from the parts list, the signal frequency at output *B* approximately equals:

$$F_b = \frac{F_a}{10}$$
$$= \frac{0.017}{10}$$
$$= 0.0017 \text{ Hz}$$

At output *B*, there is one output pulse approximately every 574 seconds, or 9 minutes, 34 seconds.

The output *B* signal is also fed into the input of IC3, which is another decade counter, just like IC2. The signal is divided by ten once more. In other words, the frequency at output *C* is equal to one-hundredth of the frequency at output *A*. Or, in our example:

$$F_c = \frac{F_a}{10 \times 10}$$
$$= \frac{F_a}{100}$$
$$= \frac{0.017}{100}$$
$$= 0.00017 \text{ Hz}$$

Output *C* will put a single pulse about once every 5,737 seconds or so. This timing period can be rewritten as 95 minutes, 37 seconds, or 1 hour, 35 minutes, 37 seconds.

The timing period can be extended even further by adding more decade counter stages wired like IC2 and IC3. A third counter stage will divide by 1000. A fourth counter stage will divide the original timing period by a factor of 10,000.

By using digital counters to extend the timing period, long timing periods can be generated with relatively small-valued resistors and capacitors. Very large-valued components such as resistors, and especially capacitors, can introduce quite a bit of instability and inaccuracy in a timing circuit.

Of course, this type of timing-period extension also can be used to create timing periods far longer than the 555/556 timer would be capable of on its own. There is no upper limit to the range of possible timing periods that can be generated by this type of circuit.

The circuit can be forcibly reset at any time by moving switch S1 to its *B* position. This will start the counters back at zero. For normal operation, this switch must be in the *A* position. In some applications, you might want to eliminate this reset switch from the circuit. In other applications, it could come in very handy.

❖ 3

Signal-generator projects

ANOTHER IMPORTANT CATEGORY OF TIMER APPLICATIONS IS THE SIGNAL generator. A *signal generator* is a circuit that produces an ac waveform of some type. Not surprisingly, signal-generator applications use timers in the astable mode. After all, the basic astable multivibrator circuit is a simple signal generator in itself.

PROJECT 11: TONE-BURST GENERATOR

The circuit shown in Fig. 3-1 can be called a "tone-burst generator." When the trigger button is momentarily closed, a burst of tone (a rectangle wave) will appear at the circuit's output for a fixed period of time.

A suitable parts list for this project appears in Table 3-1. Be sure to experiment with alternate component values. Resistors R1 through R3 and capacitors C1 and C2 are all timing components with a direct effect on the operation of the circuit. Capacitors C3 and C4, however, are merely stabilizing bypass capacitors for the timer's unused voltage-control inputs. There is no point in experimenting with the values of these capacitors, as they have no direct effect on the circuit's output signal.

Resistor R4 is a simple pull-up resistor for the trigger input. It ensures that the first timer's trigger input (pin #6) is held high when the trigger switch (S1) is open. Closing this switch grounds the trigger input, causing a high to low transision that is recognized by the timer as a trigger pulse.

In essence, this circuit uses one timer in the monostable mode and the other in the astable mode. This is made clearer if the circuit is redrawn with two separate 555 timer ICs, as illustrated in Fig. 3-2.

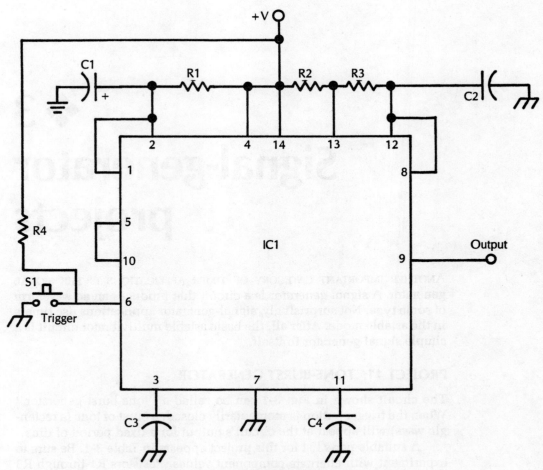

Fig. 3-1 Project 11: Tone-burst generator.

**Table 3-1 Parts List for the
Tone-Burst Generator Project of Fig. 3-1.**

IC1	556 dual-timer IC
S1	Normally open SPST pushbutton switch
C1	5-µF, 35-V electrolytic capacitor
C2	0.1-µF capacitor
C3, C4	0.01-µF capacitor
R1	330-kΩ, 1/4-W, 5% resistor
R2	12-kΩ, 1/4-W, 5% resistor
R3	4.7-kΩ, 1/4-W, 5% resistor
R4	1-MΩ, 1/4-W, 5% resistor

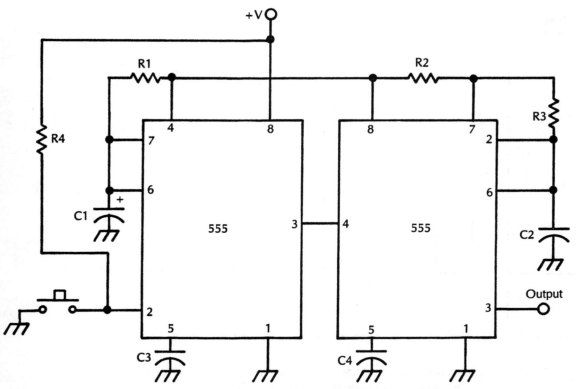

Fig. 3-2 *The circuit of Fig. 3-1 can be redrawn using separate 555s.*

Normally, the output of the first timer stage (pin #5) is low, holding the reset input of the second timer stage (pin #10) low. (The pin numbers given here are for the 556 dual-timer IC.) The second timer stage cannot generate any output signal at all under these conditions. When the first timer stage is triggered, its output (pin #5) goes high, bringing the reset pin (#10) of the second timer stage high, permitting it to function.

The first timer stage in this circuit is a simple monostable multivibrator. The values of capacitor C1 and resistor R1 determine its timing period, and therefore, how long after the trigger pulse the first stage output will be high, enabling the second stage to function.

The second timer stage in this circuit is an astable multivibrator, generating a rectangle wave. The frequency and duty cycle of this rectangle wave are set by the values of capacitor C2 and resistors R2 and R3.

Figure 3-3 illustrates typical input and output signals for this circuit. As you can see, there is nothing at all complex in this circuit. If you understood the introductory material covered in chapter 1, you should have a full comprehension of this circuit.

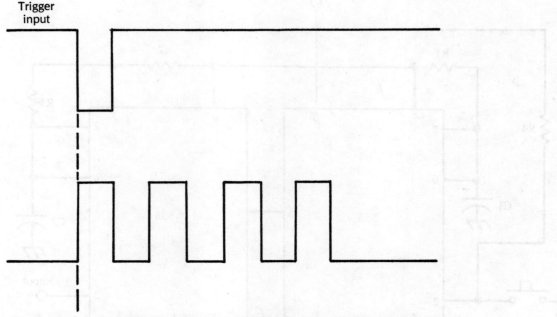

Fig. 3-3 *These are some typical input and output signals for the circuit of Fig. 3-1.*

The timing periods of each stage are determined by the formulae introduced and discussed in the general circuits of chapter 1.

The timing period of the monostable multivibrator stage controls the length of the tone burst at the output. This timing period is determined by the values of capacitor C1 and resistor R1:

$$T = 1.1 C_1 R_1$$

In this particular application, a moderately long timing period is desirable, so fairly large values are given for capacitor C1 and resistor R1:

$$C_1 = 5 \ \mu F$$
$$R_1 = 330 \ k\Omega$$
$$T = 1.1 \times 0.000005 \times 330,000$$
$$= 1.815 \ second$$

Each time the circuit is triggered, the output tone burst will last just a little under 2 seconds.

The length of the tone burst can be increased by increasing the value of either capacitor C1 or resistor R1, or both. Reducing the value of either or both of these timing components also shortens the length of the tone burst at the output, of course.

The tone frequency generated during each output burst is controlled by the timing components in the second (astable multivibrator) timer stage. These components are capacitor C2, along with resistors R2 and R3. The frequency equation is the standard equation for the basic 555 astable multivibrator circuit:

$$F = \frac{1}{0.693C_2\,(R_2 + 2R_3)}$$

In the suggested parts list, the following component values are used in this stage:

$$C_2 = 0.1\ \mu\text{F}$$
$$R_2 = 12\ \text{k}\Omega$$
$$R_3 = 4.7\ \text{k}\Omega$$

Using these component values, the tone frequency works out to:

$$F = \frac{1}{0.693 \times 0.0000001 \times (12{,}000 + 2 \times 4700)}$$
$$= \frac{1}{0.693 \times 0.0000001 \times (12{,}000 + 9400)}$$
$$= \frac{1}{0.693 \times 0.0000001 \times 21{,}400}$$
$$= \frac{1}{0.001483}$$
$$= 674\ \text{Hz}$$

Increasing the value of any (or all) of the timing components decreases the tone frequency. The tone frequency can be increased by reducing the value of one or more of the three timing components. Remember, the relative values of resistors R2 and R3 interact to determine the duty cycle of the output waveform. This influences the timbre, or perceived quality of the tone if it is fed through a loudspeaker or other audio system.

This circuit can be automated easily. Just delete trigger switch S1 and its pull-up resistor (R4), and feed an appropriate trigger signal from another circuit into pin #6 of the 556 dual-timer IC.

PROJECT 12: RECURRING TONE-BURST GENERATOR

The circuit shown in Fig. 3-4 is similar to the tone-burst generator circuit of Fig. 3-1. The main difference here is that both stages are astable multivibrators, instead of a monostable multivibrator and a astable multivibrator. This is made apparent when the circuit diagram is redrawn with two separate 555 timer ICs, as illustrated in Fig. 3-5.

The output signal will be a regular, recurring series of tone bursts. No external triggering is required in this circuit. A typical output signal from this circuit appears in Fig. 3-6.

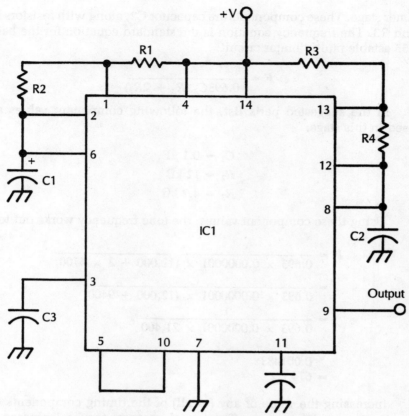

Fig. 3-4 *Project 12: Recurring tone-burst generator.*

A suitable parts list for this project is given in Table 3-2. Be sure to experiment with alternate component values. Resistors R1 through R4 and capacitors C1 and C2 are all timing components with a direct effect on the operation of the circuit. Capacitors C3 and C4, however, are merely stabilizing bypass capacitors for the timer's unused voltage-control inputs. There is no point in experimenting with the values of these capacitors, as they have no direct effect on the circuit's output signal.

In this recurring tone-burst generator circuit, the output of the first astable multivibrator stage (pin #5) turns the second astable multivibrator stage on and off with its reset input (pin #10). These pin numbers are given for the 556 dual-timer IC.

The on/off frequency of the output tone bursts is controlled by the value of capacitor C1, along with that of resistors R1 and R2, in the first astable multivibrator stage:

$$F_b = \frac{1}{0.693C_1\,(R_1 + 2R_2)}$$

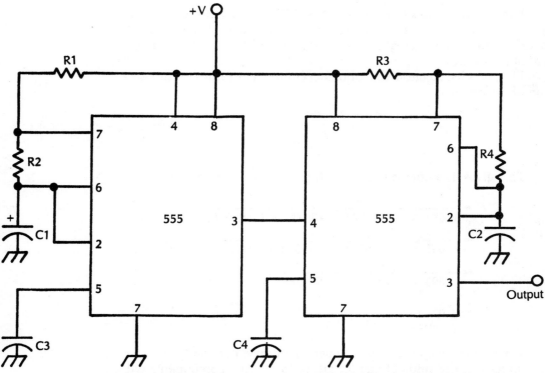

Fig. 3-5 *The circuit of Fig. 3-4 can be redrawn using separate 555s.*

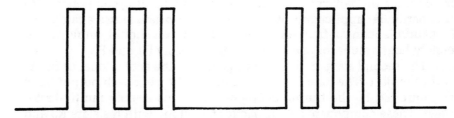

Fig. 3-6 *These are some typical output signals for the circuit of Fig. 3-4.*

Table 3-2
Parts List for the Recurring
Tone-Burst Generator Project of Fig. 3-4.

IC1	556 dual-timer IC
C1	2.2-μF, 35-V electrolytic capacitor
C2	0.05-μF capacitor
C3, C4	0.01-μF capacitor
R1	10-kΩ, 1/4-W, 5% resistor
R2	330-kΩ, 1/4-W, 5% resistor
R3	4.7-kΩ, 1/4-W, 5% resistor
R4	6.8-kΩ, 1/4-W, 5% resistor

The relative values of resistors R1 and R2 will determine the duty cycle of the rectangle wave generated by this portion of the circuit, and therefore, the relative lengths of the tone on and tone off times at the circuit's output.

The parts list suggests the following component values for this section of the circuit:

$$C_1 = 2.2 \ \mu F$$
$$R_1 = 10 \ k\Omega$$
$$R_2 = 330 \ k\Omega$$

This gives us a controlling (on/off) frequency of approximately:

$$F = \frac{1}{0.693 \times 0.0000022 \times [10,000 + (2 \times 330,000)]}$$
$$= \frac{1}{0.693 \times 0.0000022 \times (10,000 + 660,000)}$$
$$= \frac{1}{0.693 \times 0.0000022 \times 670,000}$$
$$= \frac{1}{1.02}$$
$$= 0.98 \ Hz$$

The output tone bursts will appear about once per second.

Increasing the value of any (or all) of the timing components will decrease the control frequency. The control frequency can be increased by reducing the value of one or more of the three timing components. In this particular application, it usually is appropriate to use a fairly low (subaudible) control frequency. This suggests you should employ moderately large values for capacitor C1 and resistors R1 and R2.

The second stage in this circuit generates the actual tone, as in the earlier project. The tone frequency generated during each output burst is controlled by the timing components in this astable multivibrator stage. These components are capacitor C2, along with resistors R3 and R4. The frequency equation is once again just the standard equation for the basic 555 astable multivibrator circuit:

$$F = \frac{1}{0.693C_2 \ (R_3 + 2R_4)}$$

In the suggested parts list, the following component values are used in this stage:

$$C_2 = 0.05 \ \mu F$$
$$R_3 = 4.7 \ k\Omega$$
$$R_4 = 6.8 \ k\Omega$$

Using these component values, the tone frequency works out to approximately:

$$F = \cfrac{1}{0.693 \times 0.00000005 \times [4700 + (2 \times 6800)]}$$

$$= \cfrac{1}{0.693 \times 0.00000005 \times (4700 + 13,600)}$$

$$= \cfrac{1}{0.693 \times 0.00000005 \times 18,300}$$

$$= \cfrac{1}{0.000634}$$

$$= 1577 \text{ Hz}$$

Increasing the value of any (or all) of the timing components will decrease the tone frequency. The tone frequency can be increased by reducing the value of one or more of the three timing components. Remember, the relative values of resistors R2 and R3 interact to determine the duty cycle of the output waveform. This will influence the timbre, or perceived quality, of the tone if it is fed through a loudspeaker or other audio system.

Some very interesting synthesized sound effects can be created by raising the control frequency (timer *A*, defined by capacitor C1, resistor R1, and resistor R2) up into the audible range (above 25 Hz or so). The two frequency signals (the control frequency and the tone frequency) will combine to produce new overtones in a complex output signal. This process is known as *frequency modulation* (fm).

PROJECT 13: DIGITALLY GATED-TONE GENERATOR

The circuit shown in Fig. 3-7 is another variation on the basic idea used in the last two projects (Figs. 3-1 and 3-4). In this project, the tone burst at the output is under the control of any CMOS digital circuit.

The two timer stages of the 556 (IC1) are both set up as astable multivibrators. The output of timer stage *A* (the timing period set by capacitor C1 and resistors R1 and R2) turns the second timer stage on and off at regular intervals. The timing period of timer *B* is controlled by capacitor C5, resistors R3 and R5, and potentiometer R4.

If the frequency of timer stage *A* is very low (subaudible), the output will be a series of discrete tone bursts. Timer *A* sets the length and spacing of the tone bursts, and timer *B* sets the frequency of the actual tone. If both timer stages are putting out signals in the audible region (above about 20 Hz), the signals will interact, producing a complex and apparently continuous tone with a number of fm sidebands.

Timer stage A in this circuit also is controlled by the external digital-trigger signal through IC2. IC2 is one-half a quad NAND gate chip, used as a pair of inverters. Shorting the two inputs of a NAND gate together causes it to function as an *inverter*—when the input is low, the

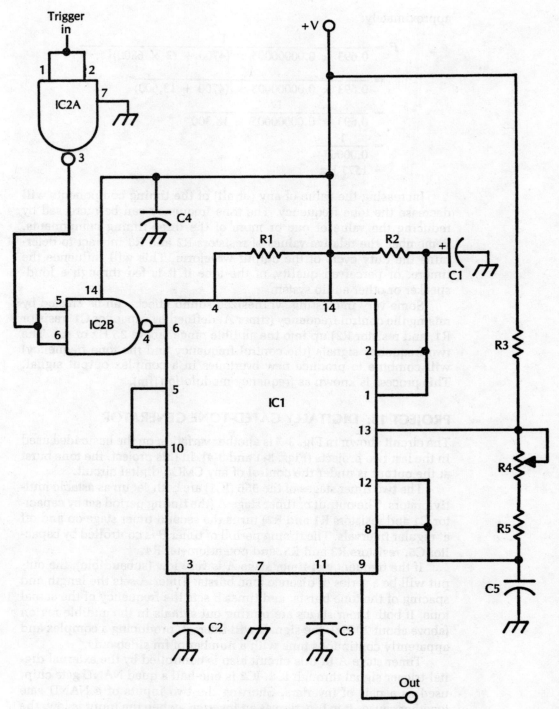

Fig. 3-7 *Project 13: Digitally gated-tone generator.*

output is high, and vice versa. By placing two inverters in series, their effects cancel out—when the input is low, the output is low, and when the input is high, the output is high. The two inverter stages are used in this circuit as a buffer, to prevent loading down of the controlling digital circuit.

The two timer stages can operate and produce an output signal only when the trigger input signal is low. If the digital signal at the trigger input is high, the timers will be disabled, and there will be no signal at the circuit's output.

Thus, the output signal can be controlled (turned on and off) by a computer or other digital circuit, using CMOS gates. One possible application of this technique would be an alarm signal in response to some digitally monitored condition.

In some applications, you might need to trigger the signal with a high signal, and use a low signal to disable the circuit. This modification is very simple—just add another inverter stage. Because there are two unused NAND gates in IC2, this modification won't even increase the parts count of the project.

**Table 3-3   Parts List
for the Digitally Gated-Tone
Generator Project of Fig. 3-7.**

IC1	556 dual-timer
IC2	CD4011 quad NAND gate
C1	1-μF, 35-V electrolytic capacitor
C2, C3	0.01-μF capacitor
C4, C5	0.1-μF capacitor
R1, R3	4.7-kΩ, 1/4-W, 5% resistor
R2	100-kΩ, 1/4-W, 5% resistor
R4	5-kΩ potentiometer
R5	470-Ω, 1/4-W, 5% resistor

A suitable parts list for this gated-tone generator circuit appears in Table 3-3. If the component values suggested here are used, the frequency of the first timer stage (A) works out to about:

$$F = \frac{1}{0.693 \times C_1 \times (R_1 + 2R_2)}$$

$$C_1 = 1 \; \mu F$$

$$R_1 = 4.7 \; k\Omega$$

$$R_2 = 100 \; k\Omega$$

$$F = \frac{1}{0.693 \times 0.000001 \times [4700 + (2 \times 100,000)]}$$

$$= \frac{1}{0.693 \times 0.000001 \times (4700 + 200,000)}$$

$$= \frac{1}{0.693 \times 0.000001 \times 204,700}$$

$$= \frac{1}{0.142}$$

$$= 7 \text{ Hz}$$

The frequency of the second timer stage (B) is manually adjustable by potentiometer R4. The value of R4 – 5 is the series combination of the resistances of R4 and R5.

Assume that the potentiometer (R4) is set to the exact midpoint of its range. If you use the 5 kΩ potentiometer specified in the parts list, this makes the value of R4 2.5 kΩ. With the other relevant component values from the suggested parts list, you can determine the approximate tone frequency (generated by timer B):

$$F = \frac{1}{0.693 \times C_5 \times (R_3 + 2R_{4-5})}$$

$$C_5 = 0.1 \ \mu\text{F}$$

$$R_3 = 4.7 \text{ k}\Omega$$

$$R_4 = 2.5 \text{ k}\Omega$$

$$R_5 = 470 \ \Omega$$

$$R_{4-5} = 2500 + 470 = 2970 \ \Omega$$

$$F = \frac{1}{0.693 \times 0.0000001 \times [4700 + (2 \times 2970)]}$$

$$= \frac{1}{0.693 \times 0.0000001 \times (4700 + 5940)}$$

$$= \frac{1}{0.693 \times 0.0000001 \times 10,640}$$

$$= \frac{1}{0.0007373}$$

$$= 1356 \text{ Hz}$$

Of course, I encourage you to experiment with alternate values for the timing components (capacitors C1 and C5, resistors R1, R2, R3, and R5, and potentiometer R4). In some applications, it might be appropriate to replace the series combination of potentiometer R4 and resistor R5 with a single fixed resistor.

Some very interesting and extremely complex tones can be generated by this circuit if the trigger signal is a periodic waveform with a frequency in the audible range (approximately 20 Hz to 20 kHz). Generally speaking, the trigger frequency should have a lower frequency than timer A, which should, in turn, have a lower output frequency than timer B. You might want to experiment and see what happens if this rule of thumb is violated.

The trigger signal does not have to be a periodic waveform. It can be made up of irregular and unequally spaced digital pulses.

PROJECT 14: THREE-WAY-TONE GENERATOR

The circuit shown in Fig. 3-8 uses the 556 dual-timer IC as a pair of astable multivibrators. The first astable multivibrator stage can modulate the second in two different ways, or the first stage can be eliminated effectively from the circuit.

The unique feature of this project is that it can be used in three different ways, depending on the setting of switch S1. This switch is a SPDT type, or half of a DPDT switch. This switch must have a center off position to provide all three of the circuit's options.

A typical parts list for this project appears in Table 3-4. By all means experiment with alternate component values in this project. You'll find you can achieve some very novel effects.

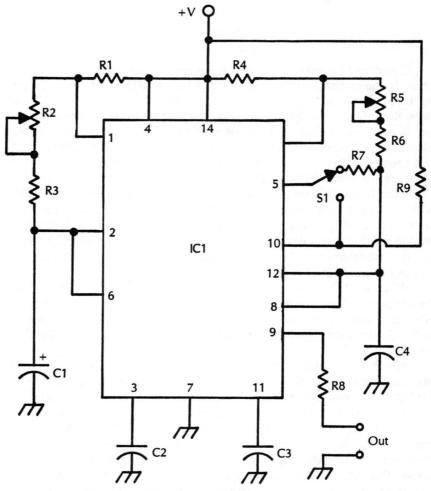

Fig. 3-8 Project 14: Three-way-tone generator.

**Table 3-4   Parts List
for the Three-Way-Tone
Generator Project of Fig. 3-8.**

IC1	556 dual-timer IC
C1	5-μF, 35-V electrolytic capacitor
C2, C3	0.01-μF capacitor
C4	0.1-μF capacitor
R1	2.2-kΩ, 1/4-W, 5% resistor
R2	50-kΩ potentiometer
R3	68-kΩ, 1/4-W, 5% resistor
R4	4.7-kΩ, 1/4-W, 5% resistor
R5	25-kΩ potentiometer
R6	1-kΩ, 1/4-W, 5% resistor
R7	100-kΩ, 1/4-W, 5% resistor
R8	330-Ω, 1/4-W, 5% resistor
R9	10-MΩ, 1/4-W, 5% resistor
S1	SPDT switch with center-off position

Counting the center off position, switch S1 has three possible positions. In the upper position, the output of the first timer stage (pin #5) is fed through resistor R7 into the timing network (resistors R4 – R6 and capacitor C4). As the first timer stage's output switches between the low and high states, it alters the voltage seen by the threshold (pin #12) and trigger (pin #8) inputs of the second timer stage. This affects the timing, and thus, the frequency generated by the second astable multivibrator fluctuates in response to the first astable multivibrator. If the output signal is fed to a small speaker or through an amplifier system, the effect will be a pulsating tone, if the first astable multivibrator stage's frequency is in the subaudible region (below 15 to 20 Hz). If the first astable multivibrator has an audible output frequency (above 20 Hz, or so), the two frequencies will intermodulate, resulting in a very complex and rather harsh tone at the output.

When switch S1 is in the center off position, the output of the first timer stage isn't connected to anything. In effect, the first astable multivibrator is no longer part of the circuit. The output will be a steady rectangle-wave tone generated directly by the second astable multivibrator stage.

The third possibility is to use the lower position of the switch, feeding the output of the first timer stage (pin #5) into the reset input (pin #10) of the second timer stage. Note that when the selector switch is in any other position, the reset input of the second timer stage (pin #10) is held high through a large-valued resistor (R9). This resistor is large enough that it acts virtually like an open circuit when switch S1 is set to short pin #5 directly to pin #10. Placing the switch in this position causes the first astable multivibrator stage to turn the second astable multivibrator stage on and off by forcibly resetting it whenever the first stage's output is low. The result is a warbling effect in the output tone.

Once again, the warbling effect is best heard if the first astable multivibrator stage is set up for a low (subaudible) frequency. If this timer stage is generating a signal in the audible range (above about 20 Hz, or so), it will modulate the second signal, generating sidebands and producing a very complex tone at the output.

Generally speaking, this circuit works best if the first astable multivibrator stage is set for a low, subaudible frequency and the second astable multivibrator stage generates a signal in the midaudio range.

The two potentiometers in this circuit (R2 and R5) permit the operator to change the frequency of either or both of the astable multivibrators while the circuit is being operated. This permits a wider range of effects. If your application doesn't call for manual frequency control, you can eliminate the potentiometers. Select the appropriate values for resistors R3 and R6 according to the usual astable multivibrator equation. (Refer to chapter 1 for more information.)

In the following calculations, I will assume that the component values suggested in the parts list are being used, and the two potentiometers are each set to the exact midpoint of their range.

The following components determine the frequency generated by the first astable multivibrator stage:

$$R_1 = 2.2 \text{ k}\Omega$$
$$R_2 = 25 \text{ k}\Omega$$
(50-kΩ potentiometer)
$$R_3 = 68 \text{ k}\Omega$$
$$C_1 = 5 \text{ }\mu\text{F}$$

If you use these suggested parts values, you obtain a first-stage frequency of:

$$
\begin{aligned}
F_a &= \frac{1}{0.693 C_1 \left[R_1 + 2 \left(R_2 + R_3 \right) \right]} \\
&= \frac{1}{0.693 \times 0.000005 \times \left[2200 + 2 \times \left(25{,}000 + 68{,}000 \right) \right]} \\
&= \frac{1}{0.693 \times 0.000005 \times \left[2200 + \left(2 \times 93{,}000 \right) \right]} \\
&= \frac{1}{0.693 \times 0.000005 \times \left(2200 + 186{,}000 \right)} \\
&= \frac{1}{0.693 \times 0.000005 \times 188{,}200} \\
&= \frac{1}{0.65} \\
&= 1.5 \text{ Hz}
\end{aligned}
$$

There are about three complete pulse cycles every two seconds.

The second astable multivibrator stage is set up for a much higher output frequency. The following component values suggested in the parts list are:

$$R_4 = 4.7 \text{ k}\Omega$$
$$R_5 = 12.5 \text{ k}\Omega$$
$$(25\text{-k}\Omega \text{ potentiometer})$$
$$R_6 = 1 \text{ k}\Omega$$
$$C_4 = 0.1 \ \mu\text{F}$$

If you use these component values, you obtain an output frequency of:

$$
\begin{aligned}
F_b &= \frac{1}{0.693 C_4 \left[R_4 + 2 \left(R_5 + R_6 \right) \right]} \\
&= \frac{1}{0.693 \times 0.0000001 \times \left[4700 + 2 \times (12{,}500 + 1000) \right]} \\
&= \frac{1}{0.693 \times 0.0000001 \times \left[4700 + (2 \times 13{,}500) \right]} \\
&= \frac{1}{0.693 \times 0.0000001 \times (4700 + 27{,}000)} \\
&= \frac{1}{0.693 \times 0.0000001 \times 31{,}700} \\
&= \frac{1}{0.0022} \\
&= 455 \text{ Hz}
\end{aligned}
$$

For purposes of discussion, you could round this off to 450 Hz, or 500 Hz. This would just require a minor adjustment of the setting of potentiometer R5.

Capacitors C2 and C3 are stabilizing bypass capacitors for the unused voltage-control inputs (pins #3 and #11). If you want to experiment with some really strange effects, try omitting these bypass capacitors and instead feeding in various dc and ac control voltages.

PROJECT 15: FOUR-WAY-TONE GENERATOR

The circuit shown in Fig. 3-9 consists of two astable multivibrator stages using the two halves of a 556 dual-timer chip, and can operate in any of four digitally selectable modes.

The selection process is accomplished through IC2, which is a CD4051 CMOS analog multiplexer/demultiplexer. This circuit is quite similar to the preceding project (Fig. 3-8), except IC2 is used in place of the mode selection switch, permitting more sophisticated control.

A two-bit digital signal is fed into the mode select inputs (A and B). A digital signal, you should recall, also must be either low or high. No

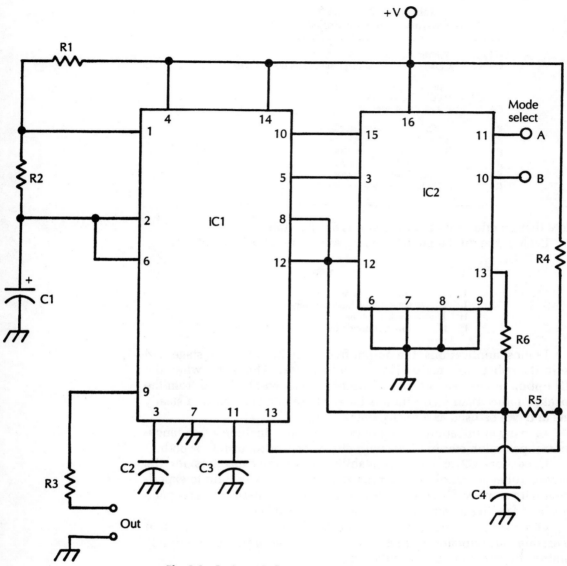

Fig. 3-9 *Project 15: Four-way-tone generator.*

intermediate states are possible. For two signal lines, there are a total of four possible combinations:

A	B
L	L
L	H
H	L
H	H

**Table 3-5   Parts List for the
Four-Way-Tone Generator Project of Fig. 3-9.**

IC1	556 dual-timer
IC2	CD4051 CMOS analog multiplexer/demultiplexer
C1	5-μF, 35-V electrolytic capacitor
C2, C3	0.001-μF capacitor
C4	0.1-μF capacitor
R1	1-kΩ, 1/4-W, 5% resistor
R2	120-kΩ, 1/4-W, 5% resistor
R3	330-Ω, 1/4-W, 5% resistor
R4	4.7-kΩ, 1/4-W, 5% resistor
R5	10-kΩ, 1/4-W, 5% resistor
R6	100-kΩ, 1/4-W, 5% resistor

Note that no other input combinations are possible.

Each of the digital-control combinations has a different effect:

A	B	Effect
L	L	pulsating tone
L	H	steady tone (second stage only)
H	L	warbling tone
H	H	low-frequency pulses (first stage) only

In most applications, the output frequency from the first stage will be in the subaudible region (below 15 to 20 Hz). Therefore, when the HH option is selected, a series of discrete clicks will be heard from the speaker, rather than a continuous tone. These clicks occur at a steady rate and can be used as a metronome.

In many applications, it might be desirable to include a frequency-control potentiometer in series with either resistor R2 or R5, or both.

Capacitors C2 and C3 are stabilizing bypass capacitors for the unused voltage-control inputs (pins #3 and #11). If you want to experiment with some really strange effects, try omitting these bypass capacitors, and feeding in various dc and ac control voltages.

Other strange and intriguing effects can be achieved by using a pair of astable multivibrators with different frequencies to pseudo-randomly control the mode through inputs A and B.

This is a particularly enjoyable circuit to experiment with. Except for the two bypass capacitors (C2 and C3), you can achieve different effects by changing any of the resistor or capacitor values in the circuit.

PROJECT 16: VARIABLE-FREQUENCY/VARIABLE-DUTY-CYCLE RECTANGLE-WAVE GENERATOR

Astable multivibrator circuits built around 555-type timers offer many advantages. They are inexpensive, versatile, and easy to work with. However, they have some important limitations.

One of the most crucial drawbacks of the 555 astable multivibrator is that the generated frequency and the duty cycle are interdependent. When you change one, the other changes too. Usually manual control is set up through a variable resistance, because wide-range variable capacitors are expensive and hard to find. Unfortunately, the same resistances in the circuit control both the output frequency and the duty cycle of the generated waveform.

The circuit shown in Fig. 3-10 shows a neat way around this problem, using both sections of a 556 dual-timer IC. The first stage is an astable multivibrator with a manually variable frequency through potentiometer R2. The value of resistor R3 is relatively small, so the duty

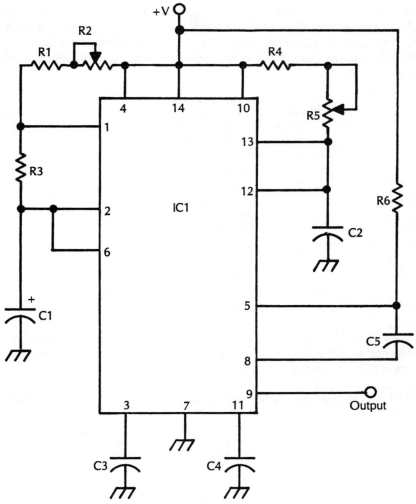

Fig. 3-10 Project 16: Variable-frequency/variable-duty-cycle rectangle-wave generator.

cycle of the generated waveform is fairly narrow, even though the exact duty cycle varies as the signal frequency is changed.

The output of this astable multivibrator drives the trigger input of the second timer stage, which is a monostable multivibrator. The output pulse length from this monostable multivibrator stage is constant, regardless of the frequency of the trigger pulses. Therefore, when the signal frequency is varied by means of potentiometer R2, the pulse width of the output signal does not change.

The actual pulse width of the output signal can be manually varied through potentiometer R5. Adjusting this control does not affect the signal frequency in any way.

A suitable parts list for this project appears in Table 3-6. As always, experiment with alternate component values. Do not make the timing period of the monostable multivibrator stage too long, however. At high signal frequencies, the monostable stage could be retriggered before it times out, causing the circuit to lock up, producing a continuous high output.

**Table 3-6 Parts List
for the Variable-Frequency/Variable-
Duty-Cycle Rectangle-Wave
Generator Project of Fig. 3-10.**

IC1	556 dual-timer
C1	2.2-μF, 35-V electrolytic capacitor
C2	0.5-μF capacitor
C3, C4	0.01-μF capacitor
C5	1000-pF capacitor
R1	4.7-kΩ, 1/4-W, 5% resistor
R2, R5	100-kΩ potentiometer
R3	1-kΩ, 1/4-W, 5% resistor
R4	8.2-kΩ, 1/4-W, 5% resistor
R6	10-kΩ, 1/4-W, 5% resistor

We will now work our way through the circuit using the suggested component values from the parts list. For convenience, we will assume that each potentiometer (R2 and R5) is set to the exact midpoint of its range (50 k).

The astable multivibrator stage uses the following component values:

$$C_1 = 2.2 \ \mu F$$
$$R_1 = 4.7 \ k\Omega$$
$$R_2 = 50 \ k\Omega$$
$$R_a = R_1 + R_2$$
$$= 4700 + 50,000$$
$$= 54,700 \ \Omega$$

$$R_b = R_3$$
$$= 1 \text{ k}\Omega$$

If you use the standard 555 astable multivibrator equation, you can find the signal frequency for this example:

$$T = \frac{1}{0.693 C_1 \ (R_a + 2R_b)}$$
$$= \frac{1}{0.693 \times 0.0000022 \times [54,700 + (2 \times 1000)]}$$
$$= \frac{1}{0.693 \times 0.0000022 \times (54,700 + 2000)}$$
$$= \frac{1}{0.693 \times 0.0000022 \times 56,700}$$
$$= \frac{1}{0.086}$$
$$= 11.6 \text{ Hz}$$

Meanwhile, the monostable multivibrator stage is using the following component values:

$$C_2 = 0.5 \ \mu\text{F}$$
$$R_4 = 8.2 \text{ k}\Omega$$
$$R_5 = 50 \text{ k}\Omega$$
$$R = R_4 + R_5$$
$$= 8200 + 50,000$$
$$= 58,200 \ \Omega$$

With the standard 555 monostable formula, you now can find the pulse width for this example:

$$T = 1.1 R C_2$$
$$= 1.1 \times 58,200 \times 0.0000005$$
$$= 0.03 \text{ second}$$

Adjusting potentiometer R2 will change the signal frequency, but not the pulse width; potentiometer R5 controls the signal's pulse width, but not the frequency.

PROJECT 17: SAWTOOTH-WAVE GENERATOR

Normally, timers such as the 555 and the 556 can generate only rectangle waves. This is generally true of astable multivibrators. However, you can be a little tricky, and "fool" the timer into generating other waveforms.

By tapping off the charge voltage across the timing capacitor, you can obtain an exponential ramp, as illustrated in Fig. 3-11. By charging the capacitor with a constant-current source instead of a simple resistance, the ramp can be made quite linear, as shown in Fig. 3-12. This waveform is known as a *sawtooth wave*.

Trigger

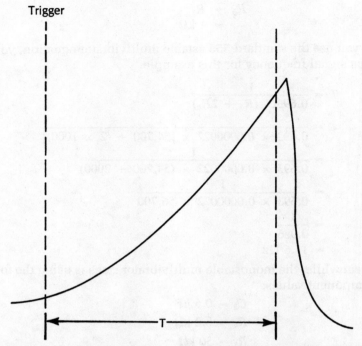

T

Fig. 3-11 *The voltage across the timing capacitor is an exponential ramp.*

Trigger

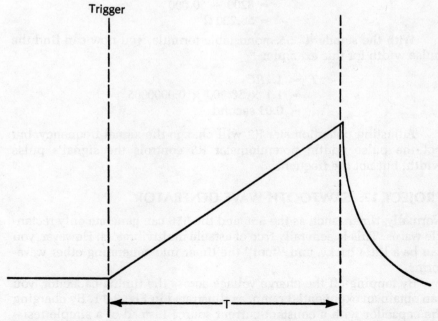

T

Fig. 3-12 *Charging the timing capacitor with a constant-current source produces a very linear ramp.*

A circuit for generating a sawtooth wave from a timer appears in Fig. 3-13. Table 3-7 shows a typical parts list for this project. You can experiment with alternate component values in this circuit.

Only one timer section is used in this circuit. The other half of the 556 IC can be left unused, or it can be used in other circuitry as part of a larger system. A 555 single-timer chip could be substituted for the 556 dual-timer IC if you prefer. Check the pin numbers as explained in chapter 1.

In the schematic diagram, the open pin numbers are for timer A in the 556. If timer B is used, follow the pin numbers given in parentheses. The power supply pins (V + —pin #14, and ground—pin #7) are the same for both of the 556's timer stages.

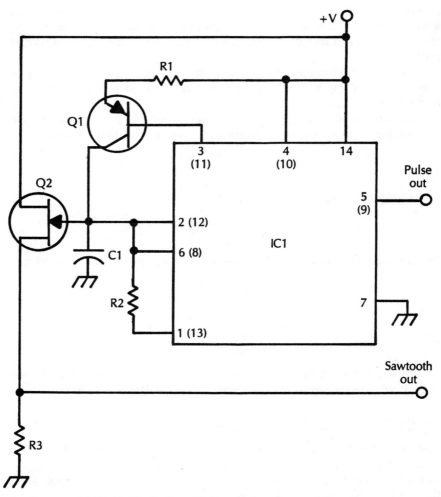

Fig. 3-13 *Project 17: Sawtooth-wave generator.*

**Table 3-7 Parts List
for the Sawtooth-Wave
Generator Project of Fig. 3-13.**

IC1	556 dual-timer (one-half used)
Q1	pnp transistor (2N3906, or similar)
Q2	FET transistor (2N4681, or similar)
C1	0.01-μF capacitor
R1	680-kΩ, 1/4-W, 5% resistor
R2	4.7-kΩ, 1/4-W, 5% resistor
R3	10-kΩ, 1/4-W, 5% resistor

Transistor Q1 can be almost any low-power pnp device. It functions as a constant-current source. Transistor Q2 is an FET, employed here as a buffer to prevent loading of the timer from the output device. Again, the exact type number of the FET used is not very important in this circuit.

I highly recommend that a + 15-V power supply be used to operate this circuit. A lower supply voltage could result in a loss of accuracy and overall stability.

Assuming you are using a + 15-V power supply in this circuit, you can estimate the approximate output frequency with this formula:

$$F = \frac{0.91}{R_1 C_1}$$

Using the suggested part values from Table 3-7,

$$R_1 = 680 \text{ k}\Omega$$
$$C_1 = 0.01 \ \mu\text{F}$$

In this example, the output frequency will be approximately equal to:

$$F = \frac{0.91}{680,000 \times 0.00000001}$$
$$= \frac{0.91}{0.0068}$$
$$= 134 \text{ Hz}$$

Bear in mind that this equation is only an approximation. Moreover, it will be less exact if a different supply voltage is used.

PROJECT 18: THE ANNOYER

The circuit shown in Fig. 3-14 is a lot of fun for electronics hobbyists partial to practical jokes. When fully illuminated, the circuit does absolutely nothing. When the light level drops below a specific, preset level, the circuit emits tone bursts (from the buzzer), separated by pauses. A practical joker could hide this circuit in a friend's bedroom. Everytime

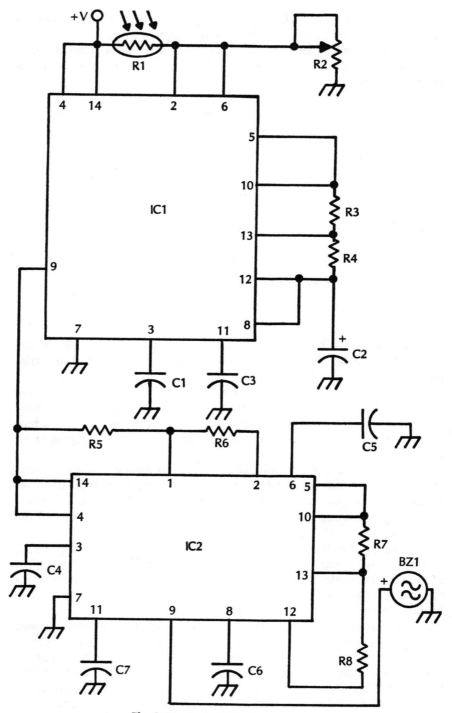

Fig. 3-14 Project 18: The annoyer.

the friend turned off the lights, he'd hear these odd noises. When he turns on the light to locate the source, the sounds stop.

A suitable parts list for this strange little project is given in Table 3-8. You might want to experiment with some of the component values in this circuit.

Table 3-8 Parts List for the Annoyer Project of Fig. 3-14.

IC1, IC2	556 dual-timer
BZ1	Small electric buzzer
C1, C3, C4, C7	0.01-μF capacitor
C2	5-μF capacitor
C5	0.5-μF capacitor
C6	0.1-μF capacitor
R1	Photoresistor
R2	500-kΩ trimpot
R3, R7	10-kΩ, 1/4-W, 5% resistor
R4, R6	100-kΩ, 1/4-W, 5% resistor
R5	22-kΩ, 1/4-W, 5% resistor
R8	220-kΩ, 1/4-W, 5% resistor

Because the circuit uses two 556 dual-timer ICs, it follows that there are four timer stages here. The first stage is wired as a Schmitt trigger.

Photoresistor R1 and potentiometer R2 make up a simple voltage divider. If the voltage between these two resistance elements is below the timer's trigger level, the output (pin #5) will be low. If the voltage between the two resistance elements is above the timer's trigger level, the output is high.

The voltage at the midpoint of the two resistance elements is determined by their relative resistances. The resistance of photoresistor R1 varies in proportion to the amount of light striking its surface. Potentiometer R2 is a trimpot that is adjusted to control the sensitivity of the photosensor.

The output of the Schmitt trigger controls the reset input (pin #10) of the second timer stage, which is wired as a fairly low-frequency astable multivibrator. When the reset pin is held low, the circuit cannot operate. When this pin is brought high, the astable multivibrator can function normally.

The output of the second timer stage controls the V + (pin #14) and reset (pin #4) inputs of the third timer stage. The third stage can operate only when the output from the second timer stage is high. Similarly, the output of the third stage is fed into the reset input (pin #10) of the fourth and final timer stage. The last timer stage determines the rate of the tone bursts and provides sufficient current to drive the buzzer.

The buzzer is a low-voltage device usually employed in doorbell and alarm applications. Select a unit with the same voltage as the circuit's power supply, with fairly low current requirements. A small buzzer will do just fine. Not much volume is needed—a little bit goes a long, long way here.

Incidentally, the author takes no responsibility for your friends' reactions if you play this prank on them. It's up to you to determine who can take a joke good naturedly.

PROJECT 19: WARBLING ALARM

If you have an application requiring a distinctive and hard-to-ignore alarm, the circuit shown in Fig. 3-15 is just what you need. It provides a loud, unmistakable "warbling" tone.

Basically, this circuit is made up of two astable multivibrators. The output of the first astable multivibrator (pin #5) drives the voltage-control input (pin #11) of the second astable multivibrator stage through a simple filtering network made up of capacitor C3, and resistors R6 and R7.

A suitable parts list for this project appears in Table 3-9. You can experiment with alternate component values.

Potentiometer R2 permits manual control of the warble frequency. You also might want to try alternate values for resistors R3 through R5, and capacitors C1 and C4.

I also suggest experimenting with the effects of changing the component values in the filter network. The relevant components here are capacitor C3, and resistors R6 and R7.

Capacitor C2 is a bypass capacitor for the voltage-control input of the first stage. Because the voltage-control input of the second stage receives a control signal in this circuit, it does not need a stabilizing bypass capacitor.

**Table 3-9 Parts List for the
Warbling-Alarm Project of Fig. 3-15.**

IC1	556 dual-timer
C1	0.1-μF capacitor
C2	0.01-μF capacitor
C3	10-μF, 35-V electrolytic capacitor
C4	0.022-μF capacitor
R1	100-kΩ, 1/4-W, 5% resistor
R2	1-MΩ potentiometer
R3	1-MΩ, 1/4-W, 5% resistor
R4	33-kΩ, 1/4-W, 5% resistor
R5	27-kΩ, 1/4-W, 5% resistor
R6	4.7-kΩ, 1/4-W, 5% resistor
R7	10-kΩ, 1/4-W, 5% resistor
R8	330-Ω, 1/4-W, 5% resistor

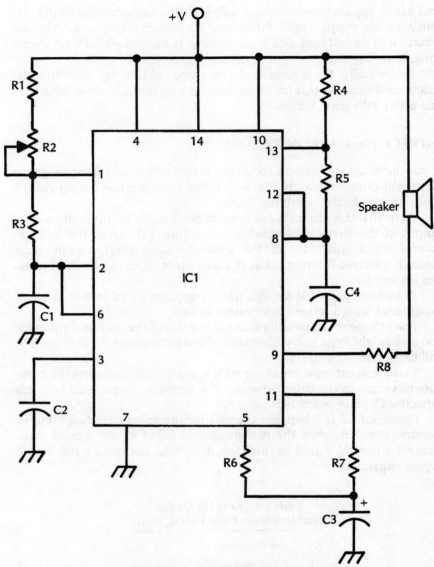

Fig. 3-15 *Project 19: Warbling alarm.*

Changing the value of resistor R8 will affect the volume of the tone produced through the loudspeaker (spkr). Increasing this resistance will reduce the perceived volume. Don't make this resistance too small. The warbling tone generated by this circuit can be really ear-piercing.

PROJECT 20: WIDE-RANGE-PULSE GENERATOR

The 555 timer astable multivibrator is versatile, but any given circuit tends to have a fairly narrow range of output frequencies. The circuit shown in Fig. 3-16, however, can cover a wide range of frequencies by adjusting just four controls—range switches S1 and S2, and by fine tuning potentiometers R3 and R6. Another advantage of this circuit is that the pulse frequency and the pulse width are independently adjustable.

A suitable parts list for this project appears in Table 3-10.

**Table 3-10   Parts List for the
Wide-Range-Pulse Generator Project of Fig. 3-16.**

IC1	556 dual-timer
S1, S2	SP6T rotary switch
C1	470-μF, 35-V electrolytic capacitor
C2, C9	100-μF, 35-V electrolytic capacitor
C3, C10	10-μF, 35-V electrolytic capacitor
C4, C11	1-μF, 35-V electrolytic capacitor
C5, C12	0.1-μF capacitor
C6, C7, C8, C13	0.01-μF capacitor
C14	0.001-μF capacitor
C15	1000-pF capacitor
C16	50-μF, 35-V electrolytic capacitor
R1, R4	3.9-kΩ, 1/4-W, 5% resistor
R2	270-kΩ, 1/4-W, 5% resistor
R3	250-kΩ potentiometer
R5	8.2-kΩ, 1/4-W, 5% resistor
R6	100-kΩ potentiometer
R7	10-kΩ, 1/4-W, 5% resistor

Basically, in this circuit you have an astable multivibrator stage followed by a monostable multivibrator stage. The astable multivibrator controls the output frequency through switch S1 and potentiometer R3. The pulse width, on the other hand, is set up by the monostable multivibrator through switch S2 and potentiometer R5.

The astable multivibrator is set up for a fairly narrow duty cycle. The output pulses from this stage (pin #5) are fed into the trigger input of the monostable stage (pin #8), through coupling capacitor C15. Each pulse triggers the monostable multivibrator, so that its output goes high for a specific, preset period of time.

Each of the rotary switches (S1 and S2) selects one of six capacitors, setting the range of each stage. Note that the astable multivibrator uses larger capacitors (C1 through C6) than the monostable multivibrator (C9 through C14). The time period of the monostable multivibrator must be shorter than that of the astable multivibrator, or the circuit will latch up. A new pulse will retrigger the monostable multivibrator stage before it has a chance to time out. Its timing period will be forcibly restarted. As a result, the output will be just a continuous high voltage, which isn't very useful at all.

It is possible to get this circuit to latch up if a small capacitor (say, C5 or C6) is selected by switch S1, and a large capacitor (say, C9 or C10)

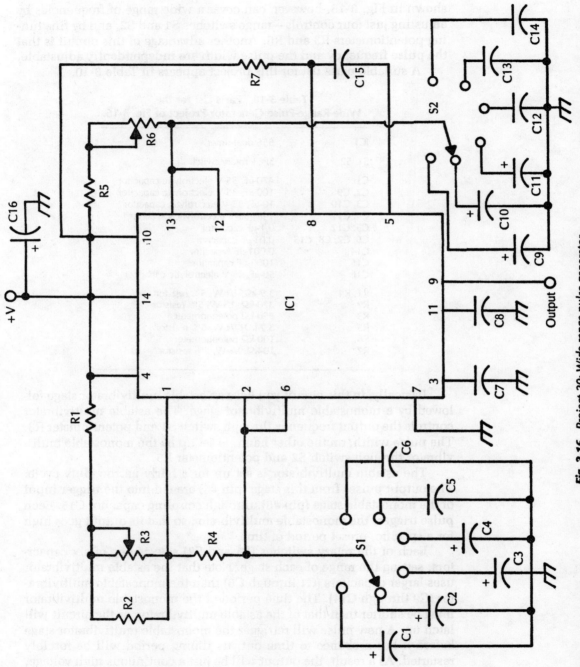

Fig. 3-16 *Project 20: Wide-range-pulse generator.*

is selected by switch S2. If this should happen, no harm will be done; the circuit just won't do anything useful. If the output gets stuck in the high state, just reset one of the range selector switches.

To give you an indication of the wide range possible with this circuit, we will work through the minimum and maximum control settings. The output frequency generated by the astable multivibrator stage is determined according to this formula:

$$F = \frac{1}{0.693C_x \, (R_a + 2R_b)}$$

In this formula C_x is the capacitor selected by switch S1 (C1 through C6). R_b is simply resistor R4. R_a is the series/parallel combination of R1 through R3. The formula for this combined resistance is:

$$R_a = R_1 + \frac{R_2 \times R_3}{R_2 + R_3}$$

You will be using the component values suggested in the parts list:

$R_1 = 3.9 \text{ k}\Omega$

$R_2 = 270 \text{ k}\Omega$

$R_3 = 250 \text{ k}\Omega$ potentiometer

$R_4 = 3.9 \text{ k}\Omega$

$C_1 = 470 \ \mu\text{F}$

$C_2 = 100 \ \mu\text{F}$

$C_3 = 10 \ \mu\text{F}$

$C_4 = 1 \ \mu\text{F}$

$C_5 = 0.1 \ \mu\text{F}$

$C_6 = 0.001 \ \mu\text{F}$

First, we will assume the minimum component values. At its minimum setting, a potentiometer is theoretically at zero ohms, but an actual device will still have about 100 ohms or so at its minimum setting. This means that the combination value of R_a works out to:

$$R_a = R_1 + \frac{R_2 \times R_3}{R_2 + R_3}$$

$$= 3900 + \frac{270,000 \times 100}{270,000 + 100}$$

$$= 3900 + \frac{27,000,000}{270,100}$$

$$= 3900 + 99.9 \ \Omega$$

$$= 3999.9 \ \Omega$$

$$= 4000 \ \Omega$$

So you will be using the following values in the frequency equation:

$$C_x = C_6 = 0.01 \ \mu F$$
$$R_a = 4000 \ \Omega$$
$$R_b = 3900 \ \Omega$$

If you use these minimum component values, the frequency works out to an approximate value of:

$$F = \frac{1}{0.693 C_x \ (R_a + 2R_b)}$$
$$= \frac{1}{0.693 \times 0.00000001 \times [4000 + (2 \times 3900)]}$$
$$= \frac{1}{0.693 \times 0.00000001 \times (4000 + 7800)}$$
$$= \frac{1}{0.693 \times 0.00000001 \times 11,800}$$
$$= \frac{1}{0.0000817}$$
$$= 12,240 \ Hz$$

The minimum component values result in the maximum signal frequency.

Now, let's see what frequency this stage generates when the maximum component values are used:

$$R_a = 3900 + \frac{270,000 \times 250,000}{270,000 + 250,000}$$
$$= 3900 + \frac{67,500,000,000}{520,000}$$
$$= 3900 + 129,808$$
$$= 133,708 \ \Omega$$
$$R_b = 3900 \ \Omega$$
$$C_x = C_1 = 470 \ \mu F$$
$$= 0.00047 \ F$$

$$F = \frac{1}{0.693 \times 0.00047 \times [133,708 + (2 \times 3900)]}$$
$$= \frac{1}{0.693 \times 0.00047 \times (133,708 + 7800)}$$
$$= \frac{1}{0.693 \times 0.00047 \times 141,508}$$
$$= \frac{1}{46}$$
$$= 0.02 \ Hz$$

The maximum component values give the lowest output frequency.

As you can see, calling this circuit a *wide-range-pulse generator* is no exaggeration. Frequencies ranging from 0.02 Hz on up to 12,240 Hz can be generated by this circuit, which is a very impressive range.

Now, let's check out the available range of pulse widths. The following formula is used:

$$T = 1.1 R_c C_y$$

where R_c is the series combination of resistor R5 and potentiometer R6, and C_y is the capacitor selected through switch S2.

Choosing the minimum component values, the potentiometer's resistance will be about 100 Ω, so:

$$R_c = 8200 + 100$$
$$= 8300 \ \Omega$$

The smallest capacitor selectable by switch S2 is C14 (0.001 μF). This produces an output pulse width equal to:

$$T = 1.1 \times 8300 \times 0.000000001$$
$$= 0.0000057 \text{ second}$$

This is a very narrow pulse.

At the opposite extreme, if the maximum component values and settings are used, the following values are obtained:

$$R_c = 8200 + 100,000$$
$$= 108,200 \ \Omega$$
$$C_y = C_9$$
$$= 100 \ \mu F$$
$$= 0.0001 \text{ F}$$

So the maximum output pulse width works out to:

$$T = 1.1 \times 108,200 \times 0.0001$$
$$= 12 \text{ seconds}$$

Both sections of this circuit offer a wide range of operating values.

PROJECT 21: TRIANGLE-WAVE GENERATOR

Ordinarily, a 555 or 556 timer used as an oscillator is wired as an astable multivibrator. This means that the only type of waveform it can generate directly is a rectangle wave. However, there are ways of "tricking" a timer into producing other ac waveforms. An earlier project in this chapter generated sawtooth (or ramp) waves. In this project, you will be using one-half of a 556 timer IC to generate triangle waves. Figure 3-17 shows this common waveform.

The triangle-wave generator circuit appears in Fig. 3-18. Note that only a single timer section is used. The other half of the 556 can be used for other circuitry in a more sophisticated system. The open pin numbers in the schematic are for timer section A. If you'd rather use timer

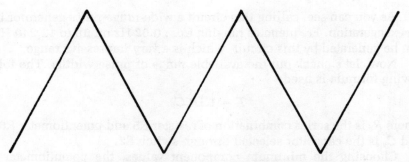

Fig. 3-17 *The triangle wave is a common waveform.*

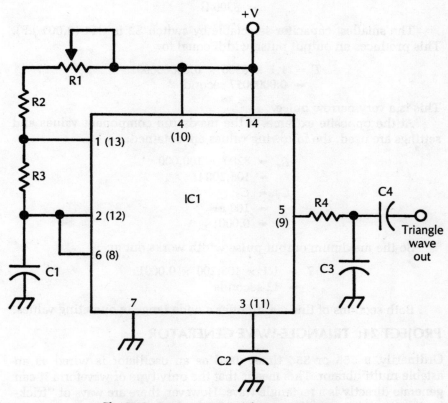

Fig. 3-18 *Project 21: Triangle-wave generator.*

section *B* for any reason, use the pin numbers in parentheses. Remember that the power supply connections (V + —pin #14 and ground—pin #7) are the same for both timer sections in a 556 dual-timer IC.

Because only a single timer stage is used in this project, you might want to substitute a 555 chip for the 556. Be sure to correct the pin numbers as follows:

556	555
1	7
2	6
3	5
4	4
5	3
6	2
7	1
14	8

A suitable parts list for this project appears in Table 3-11.

**Table 3-11   Parts List
for the Triangle-Wave
Generator Project of Fig. 3-18.**

IC1	556 dual-timer
C1	0.022-μF capacitor
C2, C3	0.01-μF capacitor
C4	0.1-μF capacitor
R1	50-kΩ potentiometer
R2	4.7-kΩ, $^1/_4$-W, 5% resistor
R3	1-kΩ, $^1/_4$-W, 5% resistor
R4	12-kΩ, $^1/_4$-W, 5% resistor

This circuit does not generate true triangle waves, but it can produce a fair approximation. Basically, the timer's rectangle-wave output is converted into a quasi-triangle wave by the output filter network made up of resistor R4 and capacitors C3 and C4.

At moderately high frequencies (several kilohertz), the output signal closely resembles a triangle wave, especially if the duty cycle is set close to 1:2 (square wave). At lower frequencies, the triangular output pulses become increasingly separated, as illustrated in Fig. 3-19. This odd waveform could be quite useful in certain applications, but it certainly is not a triangle wave.

The circuit's output frequency is determined in the same way as an ordinary 555 timer astable multivibrator. Potentiometer R1 controls both the output frequency and the duty cycle, or output, waveshape.

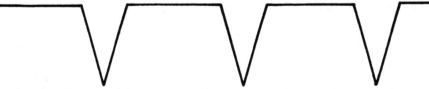

Fig. 3-19 *At low frequencies, the output signal from the circuit of Fig. 3-18 does not resemble a true triangle wave.*

In the calculations, I will assume that the potentiometer is set to the midpoint of its range. The following component values are used in the circuit:

$$C_1 = 0.022 \ \mu F$$
$$R_1 = 25 \ k\Omega$$
$$(50\text{-}k\Omega \text{ potentiometer})$$
$$R_2 = 4.7 \ k\Omega$$
$$R_a = R_1 + R_2$$
$$= 25,000 + 4700$$
$$= 29,700$$
$$R_b = R_3$$
$$= 1 \ k\Omega$$

This combination of component values result in the following output frequency:

$$F = \frac{1}{0.693C_1 \ (R_a + 2R_b)}$$
$$= \frac{1}{0.693 \times 0.000000022 \times [29,700 + (2 \times 1000)]}$$
$$= \frac{1}{0.693 \times 0.000000022 \times (29,700 + 2000)}$$
$$= \frac{1}{0.693 \times 0.000000022 \times 31,700}$$
$$= \frac{1}{0.00048}$$
$$= 2070 \ Hz$$

Try different settings for potentiometer R1, and alternate values for capacitor C1 and resistors R2 and R3. It also would be interesting to experiment with different component values in the output filter network (resistor R4 and capacitors C3 and C4).

Capacitor C2 is simply a stabilizing bypass capacitor for the unused voltage control input. The value of this capacitor is not crucial.

If you have access to an oscilloscope, it would be very handy for experimenting with this project. Monitor the output waveform as you vary the different component values in the circuit.

PROJECT 22: UP-DOWN-TONE GENERATOR

This unusual tone generator project does not produce a continuous frequency tone. Instead, the frequency goes up and down in a regular, recurring pattern.

The schematic diagram for the up-down-tone generator circuit appears in Fig. 3-20. Table 3-12 shows a suitable parts list for this project.

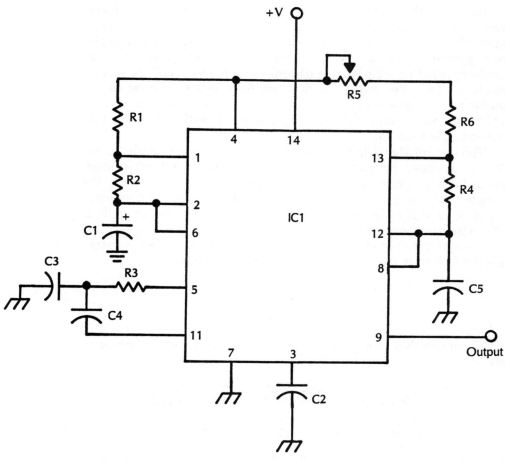

Fig. 3-20 Project 22: Up-down-tone generator.

**Table 3-12   Parts List
for the Up-Down-Tone
Generator Project of Fig. 3-20.**

IC1	556 dual-timer
C1	25-μF, 35-V electrolytic capacitor
C2, C3	0.01-μF capacitor
C4	0.1-μF capacitor
C5	0.01-μF capacitor
R1	220-kΩ, 1/4-W, 5% resistor
R2	10-kΩ, 1/4-W, 5% resistor
R3	12-kΩ, 1/4-W, 5% resistor
R4	2.2-kΩ, 1/4-W, 5% resistor
R5	50-kΩ potentiometer
R6	33-kΩ, 1/4-W, 5% resistor

Basically, this circuit is made up of two astable multivibrator stages. The first stage, which operates at a fairly low frequency, has an output filter (resistor R3 and capacitors C3 and C4), as in the triangle-wave generator project presented previously. This quasi-triangular waveform is fed into the voltage control input (pin #11) of the second astable multivibrator stage, which generates a rectangle wave in the audible range. The exact output frequency depends on the control voltage, so the output tone will slide up and down with the controlling quasi-triangle wave.

The control signal is not a very good triangle wave—each "triangle" is separated by a continuous high (maximum output) voltage, which is more pronounced at low frequencies. In this project, the triangle-wave generator operates at a very low (subaudible) frequency. The effect is still quite interesting and useful in a number of applications. Use your imagination.

Using the suggested parts values from Table 3-12, the control stage uses the following frequency determining components:

$$C_1 = 25 \ \mu F$$
$$R_1 = 220 \ k\Omega$$
$$R_2 = 10 \ k\Omega$$

If you use these component values, the control voltage frequency works out to:

$$
\begin{aligned}
F &= \frac{1}{0.693 \times 0.000025 \times [220,000 + (2 \times 10,000)]} \\
&= \frac{1}{0.693 \times 0.000025 \times (220,000 + 20,000)} \\
&= \frac{1}{0.693 \times 0.000025 \times 240,000} \\
&= \frac{1}{4.158} \\
&= 0.24 \ Hz
\end{aligned}
$$

Each control pulse lasts approximately 4 seconds.

The nominal output frequency (assuming the control voltage is zero) is determined by these component values (potentiometer R5 is assumed to be at the midpoint of its range);

$$C_5 = 0.01 \ \mu F$$
$$R_5 = 25 \ k\Omega$$
(50-kΩ potentiometer)
$$R_6 = 33 \ k\Omega$$
$$R_4 = 2.2 \ k\Omega$$

$$R_a = R_5 + R_6$$
$$= 25,000 + 33,000$$
$$= 58,000 \ \Omega$$

This gives the circuit a nominal output frequency of about:

$$F = \frac{1}{0.693 \times 0.00000001 \times [58,000 + (2 \times 2200)]}$$
$$= \frac{1}{0.693 \times 0.00000001 \times (58,000 + 4400)}$$
$$= \frac{1}{0.693 \times 0.00000001 \times 62,400}$$
$$= \frac{1}{0.00043}$$
$$= 2313 \ Hz$$

The output frequency will go above and below this value as the control-voltage signal varies.

You can achieve some interesting frequency-modulation (fm) effects with this circuit if you bring the control-signal frequency up into the audible range. Try reducing capacitor C1 to 0.1 μF or so.

Only one stabilizing bypass capacitor (C2) is used in this circuit. This is because the voltage control input of the second timer stage is being employed, so it should not be bypassed.

PROJECT 23: RANDOM-TONE GENERATOR

The circuit shown in Fig. 3-21 generates a quasi-random series of tones (different frequencies). Actually, the output is not truly random. The pattern repeats, but with well chosen component values, this will take some time, and the repetition will not be noticed.

A suitable parts list for this project appears in Table 3-13. Feel free to experiment with almost anything in this circuit. Except for the three bypass capacitors (C2, C4, and C6), all of the resistor and capacitor values in this circuit have a direct effect on the output signal.

This circuit is made up of four timer stages, so two 556 dual-timer ICs are used. All four timer stages are wired as astable multivibrators.

The first three astable multivibrators are free-running and independent of one another. Each of these multivibrators is set up for a very low frequency.

The outputs from these three astable multivibrators are reduced in voltage by some simple resistive voltage-divider networks (R3 – R4, R7 – R8, and R11 – R12), then fed into the voltage-control input of the fourth and final astable multivibrator stage (pin #11 of IC2). The diodes (D1 – D3) are used to prevent the controlling astable multivibrator outputs from feeding back and interacting with one another.

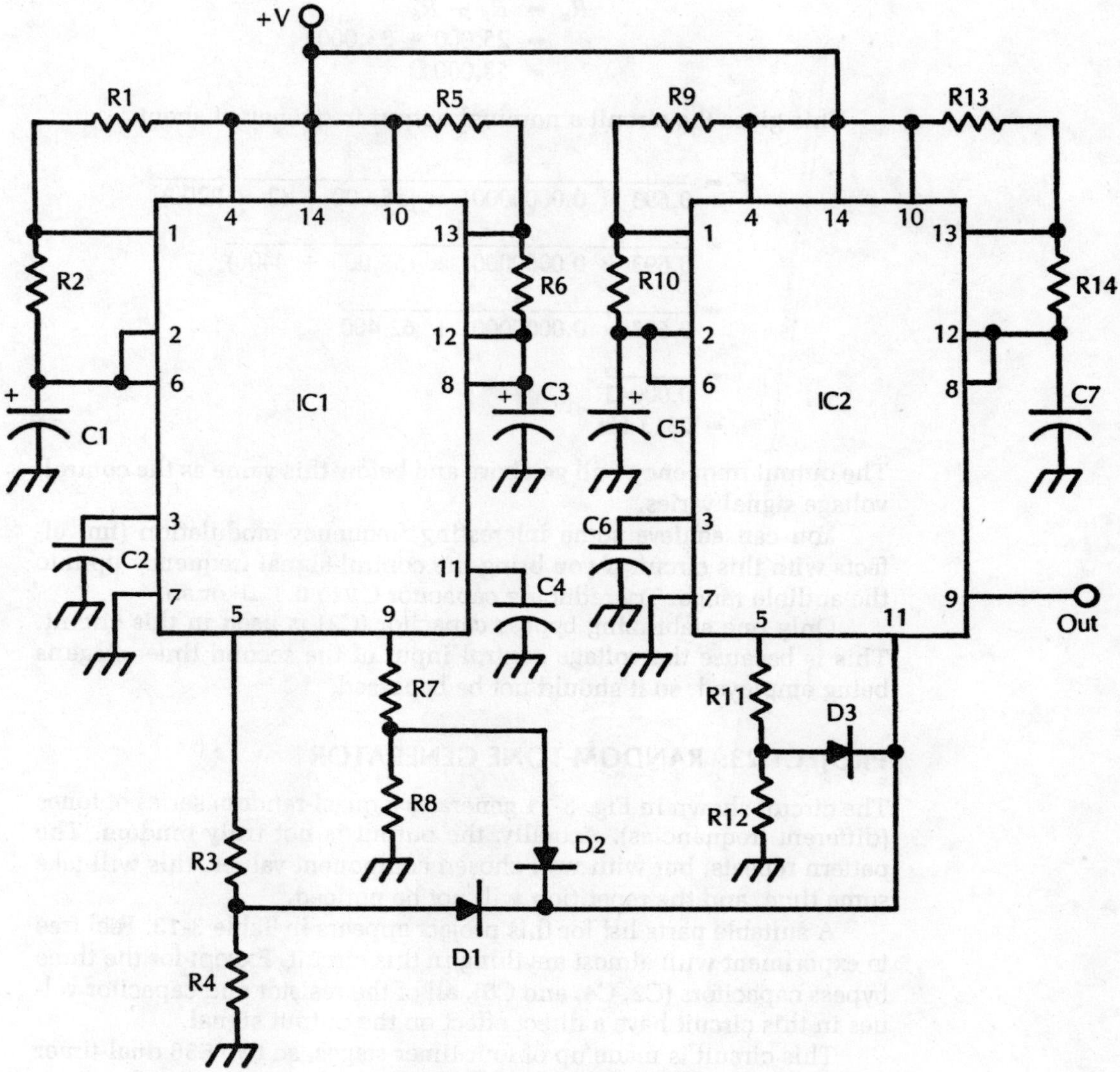

Fig. 3-21   *Project 23: Random-tone generator.*

The fourth astable multivibrator stage generates a signal with a frequency in the audible range. The nominal frequency is varied by the voltage seen at the voltage-control input from moment to moment.

The only real restriction in selecting component values for this circuit is to avoid giving any of the controlling astable-multivibrator-stage frequencies that are harmonics (exact multiples) of one another. For example, if the first stage has a frequency of 1.5 Hz, don't use 0.75 Hz (one-half), or 3 Hz (doubled) for either the second or third stage.

**Table 3-13   Parts List for the
Random-Tone Generator Project of Fig. 3-21.**

IC1, IC2	556 dual-timer
D1, D2, D3	Diode (1N914, 1N4148, or similar)
C1, C5	100-μF, 35-V electrolytic capacitor
C2, C4, C6	0.01-μF capacitor
C3	250-μF, 35-V electrolytic capacitor
C7	0.01-μF capacitor
R1, R9	470-kΩ, 1/4-W, 5% resistor
R2	220-kΩ, 1/4-W, 5% resistor
R3, R7, R11	150-kΩ, 1/4-W, 5% resistor
R4	47-kΩ, 1/4-W, 5% resistor
R5	330-kΩ, 1/4-W, 5% resistor
R6, R10	390-kΩ, 1/4-W, 5% resistor
R8	68-kΩ, 1/4-W, 5% resistor
R12	82-kΩ, 1/4-W, 5% resistor
R13	22-kΩ, 1/4-W, 5% resistor
R14	10-kΩ, 1/4-W, 5% resistor

For each individual stage, the standard 555 astable multivibrator equation can be used to find the generated signal frequency:

$$F = \frac{1}{0.693C\,(R_a \times R2_b)}$$

For the first stage, the parts list lists the following component values:

$$C = C_1 = 100\ \mu F$$
$$R_a = R_1 = 470\ k\Omega$$
$$R_b = R_2 = 220\ k\Omega$$

So the signal generated by this stage has a frequency of approximately:

$$F = \frac{1}{0.693 \times 0.00001 \times [470{,}000 + (2 \times 220{,}000)]}$$
$$= \frac{1}{0.693 \times 0.00001 \times (470{,}000 + 440{,}000)}$$
$$= \frac{1}{0.693 \times 0.00001 \times 910{,}000}$$
$$= \frac{1}{63.063}$$
$$= 0.016\ Hz$$

Each complete pulse takes a little over a minute.

Moving on to the second stage, the suggested component values are:

$$C = C_3 = 250 \; \mu F$$
$$R_a = R_5 = 330 \; k\Omega$$
$$R_b = R_6 = 390 \; k\Omega$$

So the signal generated by this stage has a frequency of approximately:

$$F = \frac{1}{0.693 \times 0.000025 \times [330,000 + (2 \times 390,000)]}$$
$$= \frac{1}{0.693 \times 0.000025 \times (330,000 + 780,000)}$$
$$= \frac{1}{0.693 \times 0.000025 \times 1,110,000}$$
$$= \frac{1}{19.23}$$
$$= 0.052 \; Hz$$

Each output pulse from this astable multivibrator stage lasts just under 20 seconds.

Moving on to the third controlling astable-multivibrator stage, you will be using the following parts values:

$$C = C_5 = 100 \; \mu F$$
$$R_a = R_9 = 470 \; k\Omega$$
$$R_b = R_{10} = 390 \; k\Omega$$

So the signal generated by this stage has a frequency of approximately:

$$F = \frac{1}{0.693 \times 0.00001 \times [470,000 + (2 \times 390,000)]}$$
$$= \frac{1}{0.693 \times 0.00001 \times (470,000 + 780,000)}$$
$$= \frac{1}{0.693 \times 0.00001 \times 1,250,000}$$
$$= \frac{1}{86.625}$$
$$= 0.012 \; Hz$$

It will take just under $1^{1}/_{2}$ minutes for this astable multivibrator stage to complete each output cycle.

The output voltages (dropped through the appropriate resistors) are combined and fed into the fourth stage's voltage control input. Obviously, this control voltage will vary in a complex pattern as the three rectangle waves go low and high at differing times. Experimenting with the voltage dropping resistors (R3, R4, R7, R8, R11, and R12) will alter the relative strength (or weight) of each of the contributing signals, as seen at the fourth astable multivibrator stage's voltage-control input (IC2—pin #11).

The fourth astable multivibrator stage generates the actual output signal. Its frequency is in the audio range and is varied from instant to instant by the control voltage at IC2 pin #11. The nominal output frequency (assuming a control voltage of zero) is determined by the following components:

$$C = C_7 = 0.01 \ \mu F$$
$$R_a = R_{13} = 22 \ k\Omega$$
$$R_b = R_{14} = 10 \ k\Omega$$

Using these suggested component values, the nominal output frequency of the circuit works out to approximately:

$$F = \frac{1}{0.693 \times 0.00000001 \times [22,000 + (2 \times 10,000)]}$$
$$= \frac{1}{0.693 \times 0.00000001 \times (22,000 + 20,000)}$$
$$= \frac{1}{0.693 \times 0.00000001 \times 42,000}$$
$$= \frac{1}{0.00029}$$
$$= 3436 \ Hz$$

This is a particularly enjoyable circuit to experiment with. Use your imagination. For example, try replacing one of the first three (controlling) straight astable multivibrators (rectangle-wave generators) with a triangle-wave generator or a sawtooth-wave generator, as described earlier in this chapter. The effect will be quite different.

You might also consider adding voltage control to one or more of the low-frequency control stages. Be creative, and have some fun with this project.

PROJECT 24: CHIRPER

The circuit shown in Fig. 3-22 generates a wide variety of "chirps" and other unusual sound effects.

Using four different ICs, this project is a little more sophisticated than most of the other projects presented in this book. Still, the circuitry is simple enough that you shouldn't have any problem at all building and experimenting with this unusual project.

Three of the ICs in this circuit are CMOS-type digital devices, so the power-supply voltage should be selected accordingly. A good supply voltage for this project is +9 volts. A complete suggested parts list for this project appears in Table 3-14.

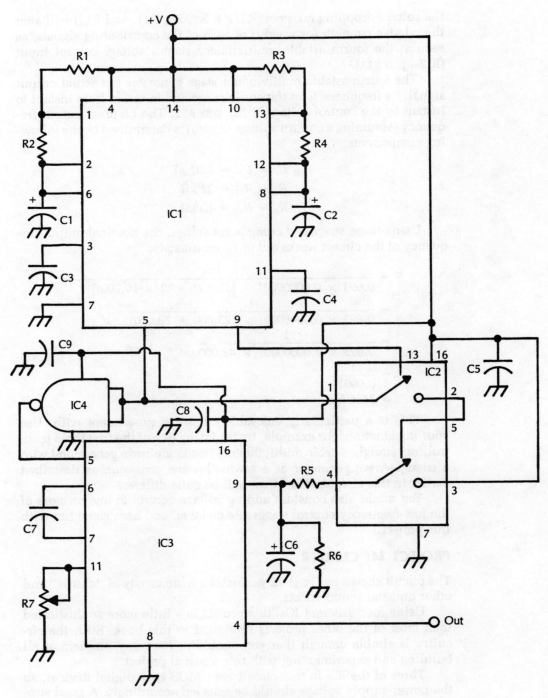

Fig. 3-22 Project 24: Chirper.

**Table 3-14 Parts List
for the Chirper Project of Fig. 3-22.**

IC1	556 dual-timer
IC2	CD4066 quad bilateral switch
IC3	CD4046 PLL
IC4	CD4011 quad NAND gate
C1	5-μF, 35-V electrolytic capacitor
C2	2.2-μF, 35-V electrolytic capacitor
C3, C4	0.01-μF capacitor
C5, C8, C9	0.1-μF capacitor
C6	1-μF, 35-V electrolytic capacitor
C7	0.0047-μF capacitor
R1	10-kΩ, 1/4-W, 5% resistor
R2	1-kΩ, 1/4-W, 5% resistor
R3	12-kΩ, 1/4-W, 5% resistor
R4	2.2-kΩ, 1/4-W, 5% resistor
R5	330-kΩ, 1/4-W, 5% resistor
R6	470-kΩ, 1/4-W, 5% resistor
R7	500-kΩ potentiometer

Capacitors C5, C8, and C9 are power-supply bypass capacitors to protect the CMOS chips from any noise spikes on the power line. Even if battery power is used, potentially troublesome noise spikes can appear because of the rapid switching of the digital gates. The bypass capacitors should be mounted physically as close as possible to the body of the IC they are to protect.

Basically, the 556 dual-timer in this circuit is wired as a pair of moderately low-frequency astable multivibrators. The output signals from the two astable multivibrator stages control a switching network within IC2 (a CD4066 quad bilateral switch). This circuit produces a varying voltage into pin #9 of IC3 through resistor R5.

IC3 is a CD4046 digital PLL, or phase-locked loop. In this circuit, the PLL is being used as a VCO (voltage-controlled oscillator). The voltage fed through resistor R5 is the VCO's control voltage. The frequency of the "chirps" heard at the circuit's output can be adjusted by potentiometer R7.

You can achieve many different effects by substituting different values for capacitors C1 and C2, and resistors R1, R2, R3, and R4. You might want to add some potentiometers in series with one or more of these resistors. A completely different effect is heard if you move potentiometer R7 from pin #11 to pin #12 of the PLL chip (IC3).

Note that the output from one of the astable multivibrator stages also is inverted (by IC4), and fed into IC4's VCO inhibit pin (#5). This, in effect, turns the VCO on and off.

You can really let your imagination run wild in experimenting with this unusual circuit. It should keep you busy at your breadboard for hours.

Try applying a varying control voltage to pin #3 and/or pin #11 of IC1. Remember to delete the appropriate bypass capacitor (C3 and C4) if you use a timer's voltage-control input. You also might want to check out the effects of changing the values of capacitor C6, and resistors R5 and R6.

PROJECT 25: CHOPPED-TONE GENERATOR

Figure 3-23 shows another unusual sound-effect-generator circuit. Once again, the 556 dual-timer IC is used as a pair of controlling astable multivibrators, driving a PLL based VCO (IC2—CD4046).

A typical parts list for this project appears in Table 3-15. As always, I encourage you to experiment with alternate component values. In some cases, altering certain component values in this circuit can have a very drastic effect on the output signal. Monitor the output through a small loudspeaker. If you have access to an oscilloscope, watching the odd patterns of the output signals can be fascinating.

The output tone is "chopped" into quickly spaced bursts. The various controls in this circuit interact quite a bit, but their functions can be broken roughly down as follows:

> R2—overall cycle time
>
> R4—chop rate
>
> R7—delay time
>
> R9—tone frequency

If you prefer, you could eliminate any or all of the potentiometers in this circuit, and replace them with fixed resistors.

**Table 3-15   Parts List
for the Chopped-Tone
Generator Project of Fig. 3-23.**

IC1	556 dual-timer
IC2	CD4046 PLL
C1	0.5-μF capacitor
C2, C4	0.01-μF capacitor
C3	5-μF, 35-V electrolytic capacitor
C5	1-μF, 35-V electrolytic capacitor
C6	0.001-μF capacitor
C7	0.1-μF capacitor
R1, R5	4.7-kΩ, 1/4-W, 5% resistor
R2, R4	50-kΩ potentiometer
R3	3.3-kΩ, 1/4-W, 5% resistor
R6	2.2-kΩ, 1/4-W, 5% resistor
R7, R9	500-kΩ potentiometer
R8	470-kΩ, 1/4-W, 5% resistor

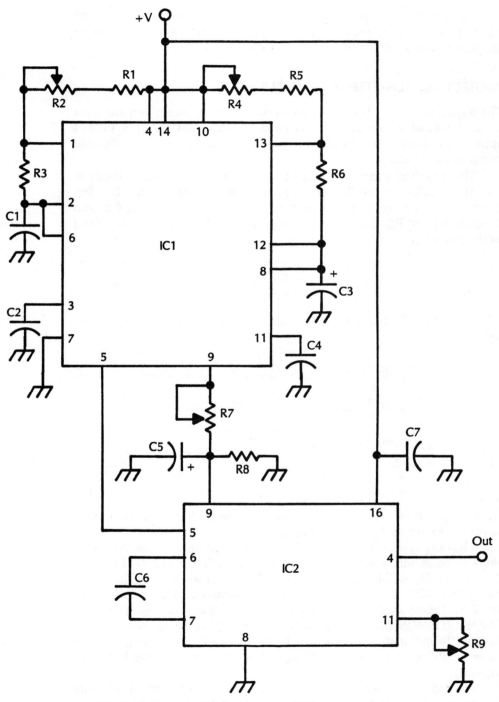

Fig. 3-23 Project 25: Chopped-tone generator.

I also suggest that you try different values for capacitors C1, C3, and C5, and resistors R3, R6, and R8. For a totally different effect, try moving potentiometer R9 from pin #11 to pin #12 of IC2.

PROJECT 26: TEN-STEP-TONE SEQUENCER

The circuit shown in Fig. 3-24 steps through a sequence of ten tones (or frequencies) at a regular rate. A suitable parts list for this project appears in Table 3-16. As always, you can experiment with alternate component values.

The 556 dual-timer is used as two separate astable multivibrators. The first astable multivibrator stage sets the sequence rate. The frequency of this stage is determined by the values of capacitor C1, and resistors R1 and R2. You will be using the component values suggested in the parts list:

$$C_1 = 22 \ \mu F$$
$$R_1 = 330 \ k\Omega$$
$$R_2 = 2.2 \ k\Omega$$

With these component values, the sequence rate frequency works out to:

$$
\begin{aligned}
F &= \frac{1}{0.693 \times 0.000022 \times [330,000 + (2 \times 2200)]} \\
&= \frac{1}{0.693 \times 0.000022 \times (330,000 + 4400)} \\
&= \frac{1}{0.693 \times 0.000022 \times 334,400} \\
&= \frac{1}{5.1} \\
&= 0.2 \ \text{Hz}
\end{aligned}
$$

Each output tone will be held for about 5 seconds before the circuit advances to the next step in the sequence.

The output of this astable multivibrator stage drives a decimal (ten-step) counter made up of IC2 and IC3. CMOS devices (74C90 and 74C41) usually will be the easiest to work with. If you cannot find these chips in CMOS form, you can substitute standard TTL devices (7490 and 7441). Both of the digital ICs should be of the same type (TTL and CMOS). If CMOS chips are used, the power supply for the circuit must be a well-regulated +5-V source. If CMOS devices are used, there is more flexibility in the supply voltage. A +9-V power supply is recommended.

IC3 has ten outputs. Only one is high at any given time. Each time the counter is advanced by a new pulse from the rate control astable multivibrator, the current output goes low, and the next output in

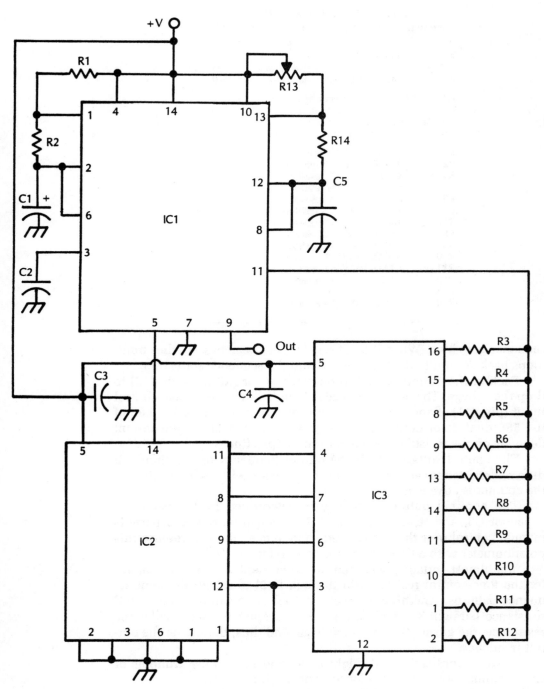

Fig. 3-24 Project 26: Ten-step-tone sequencer.

**Table 3-16 Parts List for the
Ten-Step-Tone Sequencer Project of Fig. 3-24.**

IC1	556 dual-timer
IC2	74C90 BCD counter (see text)
IC3	74C41 BCD-to-decimal decoder (see text)
C1	22-μF, 35-V electrolytic capacitor
C2	0.01-μF capacitor
C3, C4	0.1-μF capacitor
C5	0.22-μF capacitor
R1	330-kΩ, 1/4-W, 5% resistor
R2	2.2-kΩ, 1/4-W, 5% resistor
R3	47-Ω, 1/4-W, 5% resistor
R4	68-Ω, 1/4-W, 5% resistor
R5	82-Ω, 1/4-W, 5% resistor
R6	100-Ω, 1/4-W, 5% resistor
R7	180-Ω, 1/4-W, 5% resistor
R8	220-Ω, 1/4-W, 5% resistor
R9	330-Ω, 1/4-W, 5% resistor
R10	470-Ω, 1/4-W, 5% resistor
R11	680-Ω, 1/4-W, 5% resistor
R12	1-kΩ, 1/4-W, 5% resistor
R13	50-kΩ potentiometer
R14	1-kΩ, 1/4-W, 5% resistor

sequence goes high. When the last step (10) has been passed, the circuit loops back around to the first output, and the sequence starts over.

Each of the outputs is fed through a resistor (R3 through R12) to drop the voltage. The output voltage is then fed into the voltage-control input (pin #11) of another astable multivibrator, using the other half of the 556 dual-timer chip (IC1). The voltage seen at any given instant depends on the resistance in the current output line.

The control voltage affects the output frequency of the circuit. If different resistances are used, the tone frequency will change each time the counter is advanced.

The nominal output frequency is determined by the values of capacitor C5, and resistors R13 and R14. Potentiometer R13 permits manual control over the output frequency range. You can replace this potentiometer with a fixed resistor if you prefer.

You almost certainly will want to experiment with various values for the tone-control resistors (R3 through R12) to set up different sequence patterns. Anything up to about 1 kΩ or so can be used. A 0-Ω resistance (straight short circuit) is also acceptable. The smaller the resistance, the greater the control voltage, and thus, the higher the output frequency.

In some applications, it might be a good idea to use trimpots or small manual potentiometers for resistors R3 through R12.

It is very easy to convert this circuit into a complex tone generator. Just reduce the value of capacitor C1 so the first astable multivibrator stage is operating at an audible frequency (about 20 to 50 Hz). Try a 0.1-μF or smaller capacitor for C1. The ten tone steps will all seem to blend into a single very complex tone.

PROJECT 27: STEPPING-TONE GENERATOR

The circuit shown in Fig. 3-25 generates a series of tones in a stepwise manner. Table 3-17 shows a typical parts list for this project. You can experiment with alternate component values.

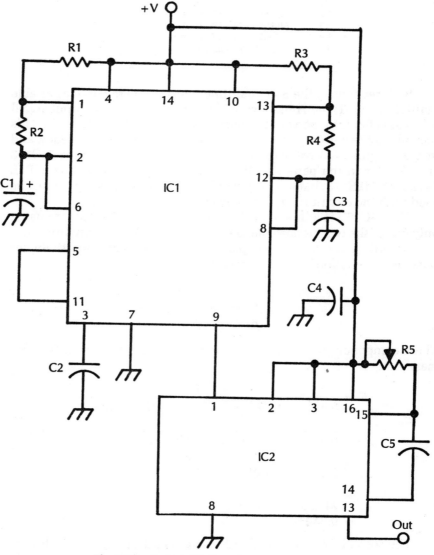

Fig. 3-25 Project 27: Stepping-tone generator.

**Table 3-17   Parts List
for the Stepping-Tone
Generator Project of Fig. 3-25.**

IC1	556 dual-timer
IC2	74C123 dual one-shot (see text)
C1	100-μF, 35-V electrolytic capacitor
C2	0.01-μF capacitor
C3	0.1-μF capacitor
C4	0.022-μF capacitor
R1	330-kΩ, 1/4-W, 5% resistor
R2	10-kΩ, 1/4-W, 5% resistor
R3	68-kΩ, 1/4-W, 5% resistor
R4	2.2-kΩ, 1/4-W, 5% resistor
R5	100-kΩ potentiometer

Both sections of the 556 dual-timer chip (IC1) are wired as astable multivibrators. Timer A has a very low frequency, and its output signal (pin #5) is fed into the voltage-control input (pin #11) of timer B. This second astable multivibrator stage operates at an audible frequency, and its output (pin #9) drives a digital one-shot (IC2). A CMOS-type 74C123 is called for in the parts list. If you prefer, you can substitute a TTL 74123, or 74LS123, but a tightly regulated + 5-V power supply must be used with the circuit if any TTL devices are used.

The 74C123 is a dual one-shot. In this application, you are using only one of the two monostable multivibrator sections within this chip.

According to the suggested parts list, the first astable multivibrator stage uses the following component values:

$$C_1 = 100 \ \mu F$$
$$R_1 = 330 \ k\Omega$$
$$R_2 = 10 \ k\Omega$$

These component values give this control stage a frequency of approximately:

$$F = \frac{1}{0.693 \times 0.0001 \times [330,000 + (2 \times 10,000)]}$$
$$= \frac{1}{0.693 \times 0.0001 \times (330,000 + 20,000)}$$
$$= \frac{1}{0.693 \times 0.0001 \times 350,000}$$
$$= \frac{1}{24.255}$$
$$= 0.04 \ Hz$$

The second astable multivibrator stage is set up for a much higher frequency, using the following component values:

$$C_3 = 0.1 \ \mu\text{F}$$
$$R_3 = 68 \ \text{k}\Omega$$
$$R_4 = 2.2 \ \text{k}\Omega$$

This stage generates a signal with a nominal frequency of about:

$$
\begin{aligned}
F &= \frac{1}{0.693 \times 0.0000001 \times [68,000 + (2 \times 22,000)]} \\
&= \frac{1}{0.693 \times 0.0000001 \times (68,000 + 4400)} \\
&= \frac{1}{0.693 \times 0.0000001 \times 72,400} \\
&= \frac{1}{0.005} \\
&= 199 \ \text{Hz}
\end{aligned}
$$

This nominal frequency will vary because of the control voltage from the output of the first stage.

As shown in Fig. 3-25, there is one manual control: potentiometer R5. If you'd like to build a more deluxe project, you can replace any or all of the resistors in this circuit with potentiometers. If you really want to do something unusual, you could use a photoresistor or two in place of some of the resistors in the circuit. The sound generated by the circuit will vary in response to the intensity of the light striking each sensor (photoresistor).

Many different effects can also be achieved by substituting alternate values for capacitor C1, C3, and/or C5. Capacitors C2 and C4 are bypass capacitors, and their values do not have any direct effect on the operation of the circuit. There is no point in experimenting with alternate values for these two components, but you can try almost anything in place of any of the other passive components (resistors and capacitors) in this project. The results almost always will be interesting.

PROJECT 28: COMPLEX-TONE GENERATOR

555 and 556 timers can be used in countless ways to generate an enormous variety of unusual and complex signals. Figure 3-26 illustrates one possibility. A suitable parts list for this project appears in Table 3-18. Once again, experiment with alternate component values.

This circuit has an astable multivibrator driving a monostable multivibrator. Each output pulse from the astable multivibrator triggers the monostable multivibrator.

Potentiometers R2 and R5 can be adjusted to generate a number of unusual effects in the output tone. You might also want to experiment with some alternate values for capacitors C1 and C3.

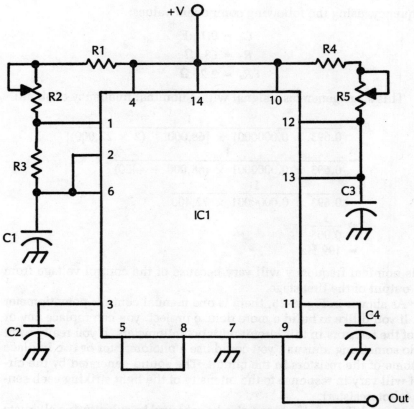

Fig. 3-26 *Project 28: Complex-tone generator.*

**Table 3-18   Parts List
for the Complex-Tone
Generator Project of Fig. 3-26.**

IC1	556 dual-timer
C1, C3	0.02-μF capacitor
C2, C4	0.01-μF capacitor
R1, R4	220-kΩ, 1/4-W, 5% resistor
R2, R5	250-kΩ potentiometer
R3	1-kΩ, 1/4-W, 5% resistor

PROJECT 29: MULTIPLE-COMPLEX-TONE GENERATOR

Figure 3-27 shows a very off-beat complex-tone-generator circuit. A suitable parts list for this project appears in Table 3-19. You can experiment with alternate values in this circuit. The possibilities are almost endless.

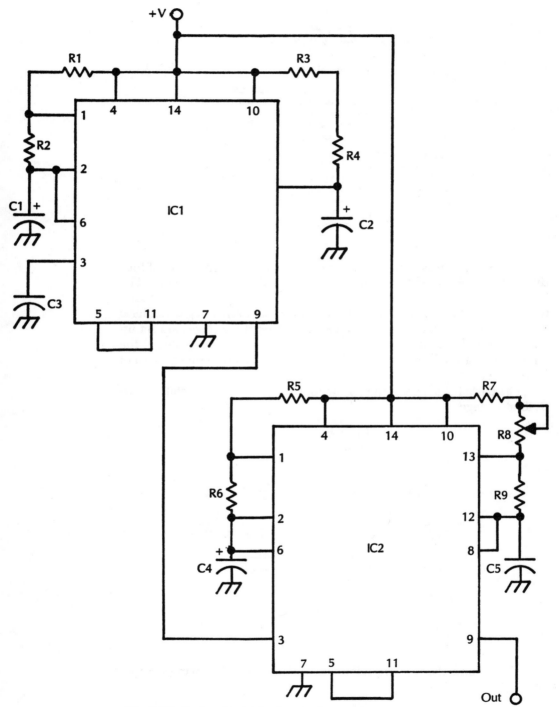

Fig. 3-27 *Project 29: Multiple-complex-tone generator.*

**Table 3-19   Parts List
for the Multiple-Complex-Tone
Generator Project of Fig. 3-27.**

IC1, IC2	556 dual-timer
C1	100-μF, 35-V electrolytic capacitor
C2	50-μF, 35-V electrolytic capacitor
C3	0.01-μF capacitor
C4	10-μF, 35-V electrolytic capacitor
C5	0.022-μF capacitor
R1, R5	100-kΩ, 1/4-W, 5% resistor
R2, R7	10-kΩ, 1/4-W, 5% resistor
R3	220-kΩ, 1/4-W, 5% resistor
R4	33-kΩ, 1/4-W, 5% resistor
R6	2.2-kΩ, 1/4-W, 5% resistor
R9	22-kΩ, 1/4-W, 5% resistor
R8	50-kΩ potentiometer

This circuit uses two 556 dual-timer ICs, giving you a total of four timer stages. All four timers are wired as astable multivibrators. The output of each astable multivibrator controls the voltage of the next astable multivibrator stage. By the time you get to the fourth stage, you have a very complex and intriguing signal. If the first three stages are set up for subaudio frequencies (below 10 Hz, or so), the tone generated at the circuit's output will fluctuate over time, producing a different pattern of frequencies.

The parts list suggests the following values for the first astable multivibrator stage:

$$C_1 = 100 \ \mu F$$
$$R_1 = 100 \ k\Omega$$
$$R_2 = 10 \ k\Omega$$

As a result, this stage generates a frequency of about:

$$F = \frac{1}{0.693 \times 0.0001 \times [100,000 + (2 \times 10,000)]}$$
$$= \frac{1}{0.693 \times 0.0001 \times (100,000 + 20,000)}$$
$$= \frac{1}{0.693 \times 0.0001 \times 120,000}$$
$$= \frac{1}{8.316}$$
$$= 0.12 \ Hz$$

The second astable multivibrator stage uses the following component values:

$$C_2 = 50 \ \mu F$$
$$R_3 = 220 \ k\Omega$$
$$R_4 = 33 \ k\Omega$$

This stage generates a signal with a nominal frequency of about:

$$
\begin{aligned}
F &= \frac{1}{0.693 \times 0.00005 \times [220{,}000 + (2 \times 33{,}000)]} \\
&= \frac{1}{0.693 \times 0.00005 \times (220{,}000 + 66{,}000)} \\
&= \frac{1}{0.693 \times 0.00005 \times 286{,}000} \\
&= \frac{1}{9.9} \\
&= 0.1 \ Hz
\end{aligned}
$$

Remember, the signal frequency generated by this stage is frequency modulated by the control voltage from the first stage. The actual frequency will switch back and forth between two values.

The third stage uses the following component values from the parts list:

$$C_4 = 10 \ \mu F$$
$$R_5 = 100 \ k\Omega$$
$$R_6 = 2.2 \ k\Omega$$

This configuration produces a nominal third-stage frequency of approximately:

$$
\begin{aligned}
F &= \frac{1}{0.693 \times 0.00001 \times [100{,}000 + (2 \times 2200)]} \\
&= \frac{1}{0.693 \times 0.00001 \times (100{,}000 + 4400)} \\
&= \frac{1}{0.693 \times 0.00001 \times 104{,}400} \\
&= \frac{1}{0.72} \\
&= 1.4 \ Hz
\end{aligned}
$$

Of course, this frequency is changing continuously because of the control voltage derived from the first two stages.

Finally, the actual output tone is generated in the fourth astable multivibrator stage. Potentiometer R8 permits the user to adjust manually the rough frequency range of the circuit. In the calculations, I will assume that the potentiometer is set to the exact midpoint of its range. This section of the circuit uses much smaller component values:

$$C_5 = 0.022 \ \mu F$$
$$R_7 = 22 \ k\Omega$$
$$R_8 = 10 \ k\Omega$$
$$R_9 = 25 \ k\Omega$$
(50-kΩ potentiometer)
$$R_a = R_7 + R_8$$
$$= 10,000 + 25,000$$
$$= 35,000 \ \Omega$$

Ignoring the cumulative voltage-control effects, the nominal output frequency works out to about:

$$F = \frac{1}{0.693 \times 0.000000022 \times [35,000 + (2 \times 22,000)]}$$
$$= \frac{1}{0.693 \times 0.000000022 \times (35,000 + 44,000)}$$
$$= \frac{1}{0.693 \times 0.000000022 \times 79,000}$$
$$= \frac{1}{0.0012}$$
$$= 830 \ Hz$$

This is just the nominal frequency. The actual output frequency will be changing continuously because of the control voltage set up by the earlier stages in the circuit. You can generate some really weird effects if you operate one of the earlier stages in the audible range.

This is one of my favorite circuits in this book. I had a lot of fun experimenting with it, and I hope you do, too.

❖ 4

LED display projects

THE PROJECTS IN THIS CHAPTER ARE ALL DESIGNED TO PROVIDE DYNAMIC visual displays, using LEDs (light-emitting diodes) as output indicator devices. In most cases, when a timer's output is high, the appropriate LED will be lit. Conversely, when that timer's output is low, its LED will be off, or dark.

Using an LED as an indicator device is a very simple idea, but there are countless possible variations on this basic principle. I will cover just a few of the many potential applications in this chapter.

PROJECT 30: DUAL-LED FLASHER

For some reason, one of the most popular types of electronics hobbyist projects is the LED flasher. This is a little curious, because an LED flasher isn't the most useful circuit around. All it does is turn an LED on and off at a (usually) regular rate.

There are, however, some practical applications for such a device. It can be useful as an eye-catching alarm indicator, or as part of an advertising display, but LED flasher projects are mostly just for fun.

I think one of the reasons they are such popular projects is that they are easy to build, inexpensive, and they do something obvious and direct. Everybody can see that the circuit works—the LED blinking on and off is unmistakable.

The circuit shown in Fig. 4-1 is a dual-LED flasher. It has two LEDs blinking on and off in perfect synchrony. When LED1 is on, LED2 is off, and vice versa. As long as power is applied to the circuit, one, and only one, of the LEDs will be lit. Both will never be lit at any given instant.

Basically, this circuit is just as simple, single-timer astable multivibrator, using one-half of a 556 IC. You can substitute a 555 timer IC if you correct the pin numbers. Refer back to chapter 1.

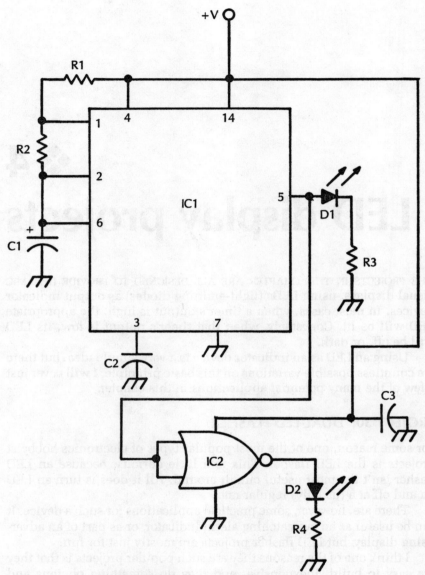

Fig. 4-1 *Project 30: Dual-LED flasher.*

The output from this astable multivibrator is a rectangle wave, of course, switching back and forth between a high and a low voltage with (theoretically) no transistion time between the two extreme states. This output signal is split into two paths.

One signal path turns LED D1 on and off. When the astable multi-vibrator's output is high, it will light up this LED. When the astable multivibrator's output goes low, the LED will be extinguished.

Meanwhile, this same signal also is being fed through a CMOS digital inverter (IC2). A digital inverter simply takes an input signal and produces the opposite (or inverted) state at the output. When the inverter's input is low, the output will be high, and when the input is high, the output will be low. The inverter's output signal is used to drive a second LED (D2).

LED D2 always must be in the opposite state as LED D1. When one is lit, the other is dark, and vice versa.

The frequency-determining components in this circuit (capacitor C1, and resistors R1 and R2) should be selected to generate a fairly low frequency of no more than about 5 Hz or so. If the signal frequency is made higher than this, both LEDs will appear to be lit continuously, although perhaps at less than full intensity. Actually, they are still alternately blinking on and off, but at a rate that is too fast for the human eye to distinguish between the individual flashes. The separate flashes of each LED all blend together, and the device appears to be lit continuously.

This phenomenon is known as the *persistence of vision*, and it is the secret of how movies work. Actually, a movie is really just a series of separate still pictures shown in rapid succession, so they appear to blend together, creating an illusion of smooth and natural movement.

Returning to our dual-LED flasher project, a typical parts list appears in Table 4-1. As always, I encourage you to experiment with alternate component values.

**Table 4-1   Parts List for the
Dual-LED Flasher Project of Fig. 4-1.**

IC1	556 dual-timer
IC2	CD4001 quad NOR gate
D1, D2	LED
C1	10-μF, 35-V electrolytic capacitor
C2	0.01-μF capacitor
C3	0.1-μF capacitor
R1	10-kΩ, 1/4-W, 5% resistor
R2	100-kΩ, 1/4-W, 5% resistor
R3, R4	330-Ω, 1/4-W, 5% resistor

Capacitor C2 is a stabilizing bypass capacitor for the unused voltage-control input (IC1—pin #3). The value of this capacitor is not essential to the operation of the circuit.

Capacitor C3 protects the CMOS gate from any stray noise spikes in the power supply line. Obviously, the power-supply voltage used for this circuit should be suitable for CMOS-type digital gates.

Resistors R3 and R4 are current-limiting resistors for the LEDs. They prevent the LEDs from drawing excessive amounts of current and burning themselves out. If you reduce the value of an LED's current-limiting resistor, the LED will glow more brightly. Naturally, increasing the current-limiting resistance will produce a dimmer light from the LED.

As a rough rule of thumb, don't use a current-limiting resistor below about 100 Ω, because it won't limit the current sufficiently, and the LED could be damaged. At the other extreme, the maximum value for the current-limiting resistor usually is considered to be about 1 kΩ. If the current-limiting resistance is made any larger than this, it will be difficult or even impossible to see the LED's glow. It will be too dim, or might not even light at all. A certain minimum amount of current is required to illuminate an LED. This exact value depends on the specific unit used. For most LEDs available to the general electronics hobbyist, keeping the current limiting resistors in the 100-Ω to 1000-Ω range is usually a good idea. Try to keep your experimenting with alternate values within this range.

The flash rate, or the astable multivibrator's output frequency, is determined by capacitor C1, and resistors R1 and R2. The parts list recommends the following values for these components:

$$C_1 = 10 \ \mu F$$
$$R_1 = 10 \ k\Omega$$
$$R_2 = 100 \ k\Omega$$

With these component values, the circuit's frequency will work out to approximately:

$$
\begin{aligned}
F &= \frac{1}{0.693 \times 0.00001 \times [10,000 + (2 \times 100,000)]} \\[6pt]
&= \frac{1}{0.693 \times 0.00001 \times (10,000 + 200,000)} \\[6pt]
&= \frac{1}{0.693 \times 0.00001 \times 210,000} \\[6pt]
&= \frac{1}{1.45} \\[6pt]
&= 0.69 \ \text{Hz}
\end{aligned}
$$

The LEDs will flash on and off about twice every three seconds (the cycle lasts approximately $1^1/_2$ seconds) using the component values suggested in the parts list. You can experiment with alternate component values.

PROJECT 31: FOUR-CORNER LED FLASHER

The circuit shown in Fig. 4-2 is a somewhat more deluxe version of the dual LED flasher project of Fig. 4-1. Essentially, there are two of the previous circuits at work here, but with a minimal increase in the parts

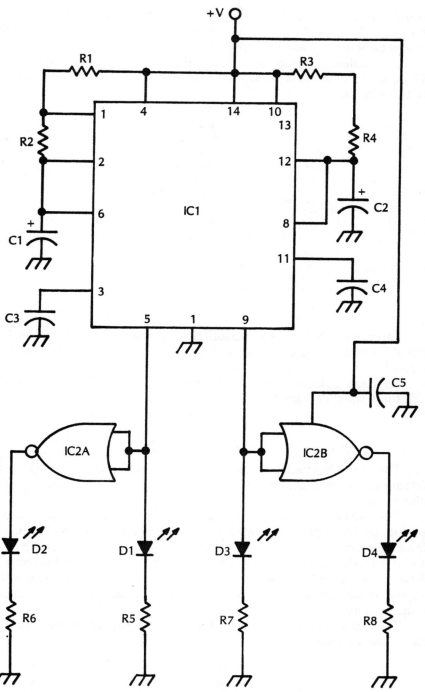

***Fig. 4-2** Project 31: Four-corner LED flasher.*

count and project size, because the 556 timer IC (IC1) contains two timers, and the CD4001 quad NOR gate (IC2) contains four gates, and you're only using two in this project.

A complete suggested parts list for this project appears in Table 4-2. There is plenty of room for experimentation with the component values in this circuit.

Table 4-2 Parts List for the Four-Corner LED Flasher Project of Fig. 4-2.

IC1	556 dual-timer
IC2	CD4001 quad NOR gate
D1 – D4	LED
C1, C2	25-μF, 35-V electrolytic capacitor
C3, C4	0.01-μF capacitor
C5	0.1-μF capacitor
R1, R3	6.8-kΩ, 1/4-W, 5% resistor
R2, R4	33-kΩ, 1/4-W, 5% resistor
R5 – R8	330-Ω, 1/4-W, 5% resistor

Capacitors C3 and C4 are stabilizing bypass capacitors, and resistors R5 through R8 are current-limiting resistors for the four LEDs (D1 through D4).

Personally, I feel the best way to use this circuit is to mount the four LEDs in a square shape, like this:

D1   D4

D3   D2

The LEDs diagonally across from each other (D1 and D2, or D3 and D4) are always in opposite states. When one is lit, the other is dark, and vice versa.

The two astable multivibrators are entirely independent and can be set for any frequency, but I think it is most interesting to use the same frequency-determining component values in both halves of the circuit. The two timers will not be quite synchronized because of random phase differences and minor errors in component tolerances. The LEDs will appear to flash almost, but not quite, at the same time. The effect can be quite hypnotic.

The parts list for this project recommends the following component values for the timing components:

$$C_1 = 25 \ \mu\text{F}$$
$$R_1 = 6.98 \ \text{k}\Omega$$
$$R_2 = 33 \ \text{k}\Omega$$

This gives each half of the circuit a nominal frequency of:

$$F = \frac{1}{0.693 \times 0.000025 \times [6800 + (2 \times 33,000)]}$$

$$= \frac{1}{0.693 \times 0.0000025 \times (6800 + 66,000)}$$

$$= \frac{1}{0.693 \times 0.0000025 \times 72,800}$$

$$= \frac{1}{1.26}$$

$$= 0.79 \text{ Hz}$$

Each of the four LEDs will flash on and off about once every $1^{1}/_{4}$ seconds, but they will not be synchronized with one another. They will not flash on and off together, even though they nominally flash at the same rate. Watching this project in action is a lot more interesting than it sounds.

PROJECT 32: SEQUENTIAL FLASHER

The circuit shown in Fig. 4-3 uses four monostable multivibrators in series. Each stage operates its own individual LED and triggers the next stage in line.

In operation, when the circuit is triggered, LED D1 immediately comes on for a period determined by the values of resistor R1 and capacitor C1. Then LED D1 will go dark, and LED D2 will light up. After a time period set by resistor R2 and capacitor C2, D2 is extinguished, and LED D3 turns on. This stage's timing period is controlled by resistor R7 and capacitor C5. When this stage times out, D3 goes off, and D4 comes on. LED D4 stays on for a period set by the values of resistor R8 and capacitor C6. It then turns off again, and all four LEDs stay dark until the circuit receives another incoming trigger pulse.

A suitable parts list for this project appears in Table 4-3.

Table 4-3 Parts List for the Sequential Flasher Project of Fig. 4-3.

IC1	556 dual-timer
D1 – D4	LED
C1, C5	50-µF, 35-V electrolytic capacitor
C2, C6	10-µF, 35-V electrolytic capacitor
C3, C4, C7, C8	0.01-µF capacitor
R1	470-kΩ, 1/4-W, 5% resistor
R2	330-kΩ, 1/4-W, 5% resistor
R3, R5, R6, R9	330-Ω, 1/4-W, 5% resistor
R4, R8	1-MΩ, 1/4-W, 5% resistor
R7	220-kΩ, 1/4-W, 5% resistor

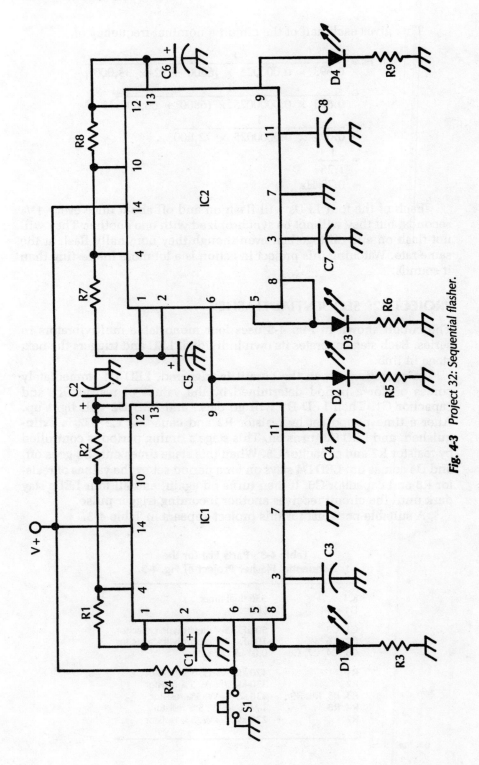

Fig. 4-3 Project 32: Sequential flasher.

This project is very similar to the Four-Stage-Sequential Timer project presented in chapter 2. You might want to refer to that section for more information on how the circuitry works.

You can experiment with alternate component values, particularly the eight timing components. Generally, this type of circuit will be most useful with moderate to long timing periods for each stage.

Each stage is just a basic 555 timer monostable multivibrator, so the standard equation is used:

$$T = 1.1RC$$

If you use the component values suggested in the parts list, the first stage will have a timing period of about:

$$C_1 = 50 \ \mu F$$
$$R_1 = 470 \ k\Omega$$
$$T = 1.1 \times 470,000 \times 0.00005$$
$$= 25.85 \ seconds$$

The second stage has the following timing period:

$$C_2 = 10 \ \mu F$$
$$R_2 = 330 \ k\Omega$$
$$T = 1.1 \times 330,000 \times 0.00001$$
$$= 3.63 \ seconds$$

Moving on to the third stage, its timing period works out to:

$$C_5 = 25 \ \mu F$$
$$R_7 = 220 \ k\Omega$$
$$T = 1.1 \times 220,000 \times 0.000025$$
$$= 6.05 \ seconds$$

Finally, the fourth and last stage has the following timing period:

$$C_6 = 10 \mu F$$
$$R_8 = 1 \ M\Omega$$
$$T = 1.1 \times 1,000,000 \times 0.00001$$
$$= 11 \ seconds$$

Of course, different component values will produce different timing periods for each of the stages in this circuit.

PROJECT 33: LED LIGHT-CHASER DISPLAY

Figure 4-4 illustrates another sequential-LED-flasher circuit. Table 4-4 shows the parts list. This circuit features twenty LEDs that are lit sequentially, two at a time.

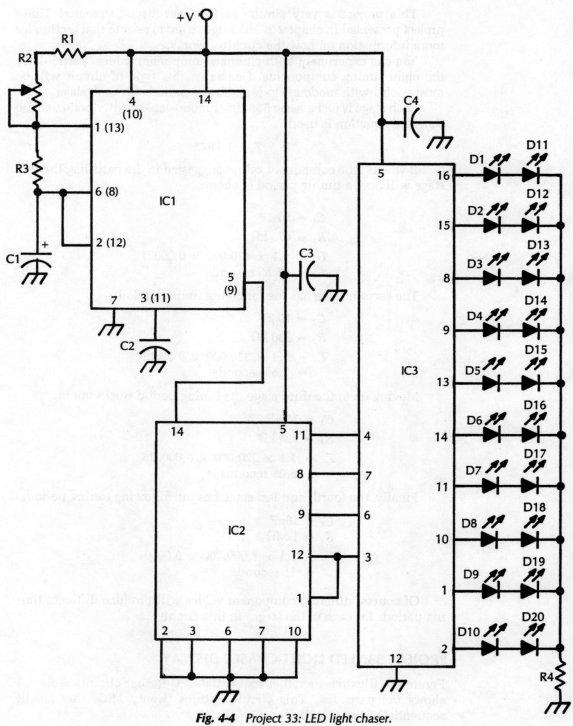

Fig. 4-4 Project 33: LED light chaser.

**Table 4-4   Parts List for the
LED Light Chaser Project of Fig. 4-4.**

IC1	556 dual-timer
IC2	74C90 BCD decade counter (see text)
IC3	74C41 BCD-to-decimal decoder (see text)
D1 – D20	LED
C1	10-μF, 35-V electrolytic capacitor
C2	0.01-μF capacitor
C3, C4	0.1-μF capacitor
R1	22-kΩ, 1/4-W, 5% resistor
R2	100-kΩ potentiometer
R3	1-kΩ, 1/4-W, 5% resistor
R4	220-Ω, 1/4-W, 5% resistor

Only one-half of the 556 dual-timer (IC1) is used in this circuit. If you prefer to use timer stage B, use the pin numbers given in parentheses. A 555 single-timer IC could be substituted, if you prefer. Refer back to chapter 1 to renumber the pin connections.

The timer is wired as an astable multivibrator, serving as a low-frequency clock to advance the sequence. On each clock pulse, the current LEDs go dark, and the next LEDs in line light up.

The parts list offers the following suggestions for the timing components within the astable multivibrator stage. (I will assume the potentiometer (R2) is set to the midpoint of its range):

$$C_1 = 10 \ \mu F$$
$$R_1 = 22 \ k\Omega$$
$$R_2 = 50 \ k\Omega \ (100\text{-}k\Omega \ \text{potentiometer})$$
$$R_3 = 1 \ k\Omega$$
$$R_a = R_1 + R_2$$
$$= 22,000 + 50,000$$
$$= 72,0009 \ \Omega$$

With these component values, the clock frequency works out to approximately:

$$F = \frac{1}{0.693 \times 0.00001 \times [72,000 + (2 \times 1000)]}$$
$$= \frac{1}{0.693 \times 0.00001 \times (72,000 + 2000)}$$
$$= \frac{1}{0.693 \times 0.00001 \times 74,000}$$
$$= \frac{1}{0.51}$$
$$= 1.95 \ Hz$$

Each clock pulse lasts approximately $^1/_2$ a second. Of course, I encourage you to experiment with alternate component values.

The output of the astable multivibrator drives a ten-step digital counter, made up of IC2 and IC3. The parts list recommends the CMOS versions—74C90 (BCD decade counter) and 74C41 (BCD-to-decimal decoder). If you have trouble finding these chips, you could substitute the standard TTL versions—7490 and 7441. If TTL devices are used, the circuit's power supply must be a well-regulated + 5-V source. TTL gates are very fussy about their supply voltage. Both IC2 and IC3 must be the same type; that is, they must both be CMOS, or they must be TTL. Do not mix logic families in this circuit.

IC3 has ten separate output lines. Only one output is high at any given moment. All other outputs are low. The high output indicates the current count value. When the count cycle is completed, it jumps back to the beginning (count of zero), and starts over.

Each of the ten counter outputs drive two LEDs in series. Naturally, both LEDs in a given output line must always operate in unison. Because only one output is ever activated at any given instant, a single current-limiting resistor (R4) can be used to protect all 20 LEDs. If you would like the LEDs to glow a little brighter, try reducing the value of resistor R4, but do not go below 90 Ω.

The LEDs should be arranged in a large circle in numerical order, as shown in Fig. 4-5. If you prefer, you could use some other closed shape, such as a square, or a triangle. The important point is to keep the LEDs in the correct order.

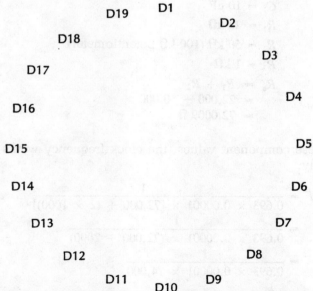

Fig. 4-5 *The LEDs in the circuit of Fig. 4-4 should be arranged in a circular pattern, in numerical order.*

In operation, two lights will appear to be moving around the circle (or other shape). The two moving lights seem to be chasing each other, so this type of circuit is often known as a *light chaser*.

TWO-RATE FLASHER

The circuit shown in Fig. 4-6 flashes two LEDs at different, but synchronized, rates. The LEDs both come on at the same time, but the time they remain lit differs.

A suitable parts list for this project appears in Table 4-5. As always, I encourage you to experiment with alternate component values.

Basically, this circuit is just a variation on an idea that has been used in several other projects in this book. One timer section is wired as

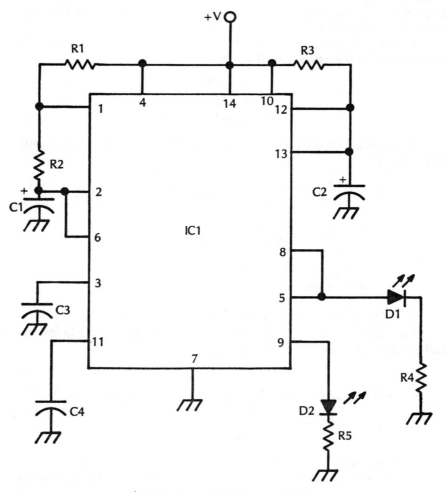

Fig. 4-6 *Project 34: Two-rate flasher.*

**Table 4-5 Parts List for the
Two-Rate Flasher Project of Fig. 4-6.**

IC1	556 dual-timer
D1, D2	LED
C1	33-μF, 35-V electrolytic capacitor
C2	10-μF, 35-V electrolytic capacitor
C3, C4	0.01-μF capacitor
R1	220-kΩ, 1/4-W, 5% resistor
R2	10-kΩ, 1/4-W, 5% resistor
R3	100-kΩ, 1/4-W, 5% resistor
R4, R5	330-Ω, 1/4-W, 5% resistor

an astable multivibrator. This stage drives LED D1 directly, and also triggers the second stage, which is a monostable multivibrator. The output of the monostable multivibrator stage drives LED D2.

According to the suggested parts list, the following component values are used in the astable multivibrator stage:

$$C_1 = 33 \ \mu F$$
$$R_1 = 220 \ k\Omega$$
$$R_2 = 10 \ k\Omega$$

This means that the flash rate for the LEDs in this circuit works out to approximately:

$$F = \frac{1}{0.693 \times 0.000033 \times [220,000 + (2 \times 10,000)]}$$
$$= \frac{1}{0.693 \times 0.000033 \times 240,000}$$
$$= \frac{1}{5.5}$$
$$= 0.18 \ Hz$$

The LEDs flash about once every 5 1/2 seconds.

How long does LED D1 stay on for each flash? The formula for the high portion of an astable multivibrator's cycle is:

$$T_h = 0.693 R_2 C_1$$

So, in this example, each flash of LED D1 lasts approximately:

$$T_h = 0.693 \times 10,000 \times 0.000033$$
$$= 0.23 \ second$$

Each of LED D1's flashes last about a quarter of a second.

The length of the flashes produced by LED D2 is determined by the monostable multivibrator stage, which uses the following component values (from the suggested parts list:

$$C_2 = 10 \ \mu F$$
$$R_3 = 330 \ k\Omega$$

These component values yield a timing period of approximately:

$$T = 1.1 \times 330,000 \times 0.00001$$
$$= 2.3 \text{ seconds}$$

Each flash of LED D2 lasts a little over two seconds.

With the component values outlined in the suggested parts list, both LEDs will come on every 5½ seconds. LED D1 will stay lit for about ¼ second, and LED D2 will stay lit for about 2 seconds. This pattern will repeat for as long as power is applied to the circuit.

Experiment with alternate component values. The only restriction is that the timing period of the monostable multivibrator stage should be longer than the high time portion of the astable multivibrator stage's cycle.

PROJECT 35: FLUCTUATING FLASHER

Most LED flasher circuits operate at a uniform rate. The LED flashes every x seconds. Each flash lasts the same amount of time, and there is always the same pause between flashes.

This is not true of the LED flasher circuit shown in Fig. 4-7. The flash rate fluctuates, creating a more irregular pattern.

Table 4-6 shows a typical parts list for this project. As always, I encourage you to experiment with alternate component values in this circuit.

In this circuit, the 556 dual-timer is being used as two astable multivibrator stages. The output from the first stage (pin #5) is fed into the control voltage input of the second stage (pin #11). This means the output frequency from the second astable multivibrator stage fluctuates

Table 4-6 Parts List for the Fluctuating Flasher Project of Fig. 4-7.

IC1	556 dual-timer
C1	25-μF, 35-V electrolytic capacitor
C2	10-μF, 35-V electrolytic capacitor
C3	0.01-μF capacitor
R1	100-kΩ, ¼-W, 5% resistor
R2	220-kΩ, ¼-W, 5% resistor
R3	270-kΩ, ¼-W, 5% resistor
R4	68-kΩ, ¼-W, 5% resistor
R5	330-Ω, ¼-W, 5% resistor

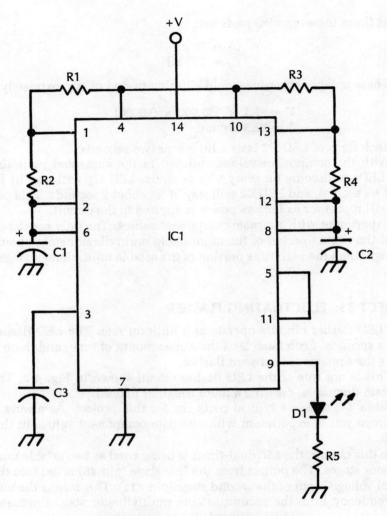

Fig. 4-7 *Project 35: Fluctuating flasher.*

over time. The output signal from the second (modulated) astable multivibrator stage is used to drive the LED (D1).

For the best results, both astable multivibrator stages should be operated at very low (subaudio) frequencies. Generally speaking, frequencies below 10 Hz, or even lower, should be used in both stages of this circuit.

The parts list suggests the following values for the first astable multivibrator stage:

$$C_1 = 25 \ \mu\text{F}$$
$$R_1 = 100 \ \text{k}\Omega$$
$$R_2 = 220 \ \text{k}\Omega$$

With these values, the modulating frequency in this circuit works out to about:

$$F = \frac{1}{0.693 \times 0.000025 \times [100,000 + (2 \times 220,000)]}$$

$$= \frac{1}{0.693 \times 0.000025 \times (100,000 + 440,000)}$$

$$= \frac{1}{0.693 \times 0.000025 \times 540,000}$$

$$= \frac{1}{9.35}$$

$$= 0.1 \text{ Hz}$$

This astable multivibrator stage has a cycle length of a little over 9 seconds.

For the second astable multivibrator stage, the following component values are suggested in the parts list:

$$C_1 = 10 \ \mu F$$
$$R_3 = 270 \ k\Omega$$
$$R_4 = 68 \ k\Omega$$

This means that (ignoring the voltage-control effects) the output of this stage, and thus, the LED's flash rate, is nominally equal to about:

$$F = \frac{1}{0.693 \times 0.00001 \times [270,000 + (2 \times 68,000)]}$$

$$= \frac{1}{0.693 \times 0.00001 \times (270,000 + 136,000)}$$

$$= \frac{1}{0.693 \times 0.00001 \times 406,000}$$

$$= \frac{1}{2.8}$$

$$= 0.35 \text{ Hz}$$

If you ignore the effects of the voltage-control signal from the first stage, the LED will flash about once every three seconds, or so. As the second stage is modulated by the first stage, the flash rate will fluctuate.

You can experiment with other component values in this circuit. Generally speaking, the best results will be obtained if the first astable multivibrator stage has a lower frequency than the second astable multivibrator stage.

Capacitor C3 is a stabilizing bypass capacitor for the unused voltage-control input (pin #3) of the first timer stage. It's value is not crucial, and does not affect directly the operation of the circuit.

Note that because the voltage-control input occurs in the second stage, this stage does not call for a bypass capacitor.

PROJECT 36: QUASI-RANDOM FOUR-WAY FLASHER

The circuit shown in Fig. 4-8 flashes four LEDs in a seemingly random fashion. Actually, there is a pattern that eventually will repeat, but it is a long, irregular pattern, so the repetition will not be obvious.

A suitable parts list for this project appears in Table 4-7. As with most of the projects in this book, it will be worth your while to experiment with alternate component values in this circuit.

The 556 dual-timer (IC1) is used in this circuit as a pair of independent astable multivibrators. These two astable multivibrators are designed to operate at different frequencies. The two signal frequencies should not be related harmonically (exact multiples of one another). That is, if timer A is generating a frequency of 2 Hz, you should not set up timer B to generate 1 Hz, 4 Hz, of 6 Hz. Instead, try something like 3.25 Hz for the second astable multivibrator stage.

Although I encourage you to experiment with alternate component values, the parts list recommends the following component values for the first astable multivibrator stage in this circuit:

$$C_1 = 10 \ \mu F$$
$$R_1 = 100 \ k\Omega$$
$$R_2 = 47 \ k\Omega$$

With these component values, the first astable multivibrator stage generates a signal frequency of approximately:

$$F = \frac{1}{0.693 \times 0.00001 \times [100,000 + (2 \times 47,000)]}$$
$$= \frac{1}{0.693 \times 0.00001 \times (100,000 + 94,000)}$$
$$= \frac{1}{0.693 \times 0.00001 \times 194,000}$$
$$= \frac{1}{1.34}$$
$$= 0.74 \ Hz$$

The second astable multivibrator stage uses the following suggested component values:

$$C_2 = 25 \ \mu F$$
$$R_3 = 82 \ k\Omega$$
$$R_4 = 220 \ k\Omega$$

With these component values, the second astable multivibrator

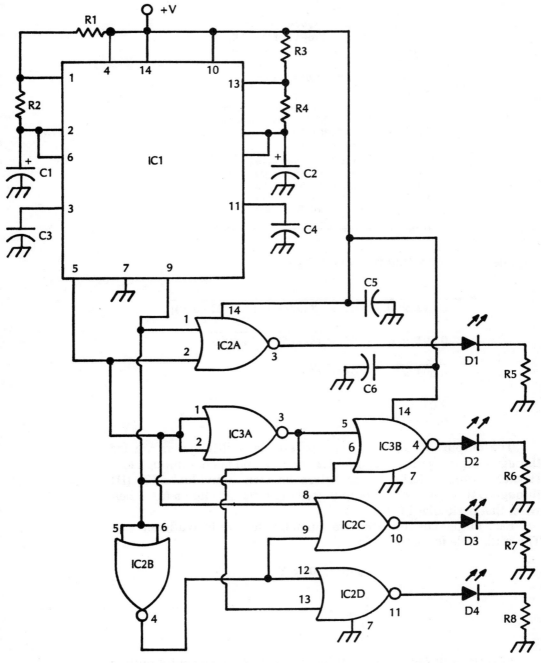

Fig. 4-8 *Project 36: Quasi-random four-way flasher.*

Table 4-7
Parts List for the Quasi-Random
Four-Way Flasher Project of Fig. 4-8.

IC1	556 dual-timer
IC2, IC3	CD4001 quad NOR gate
D1–D4	LED
C1	10-μF, 35-V electrolytic capacitor
C2	25-μF, 35-V electrolytic capacitor
C3, C4	0.01-μF capacitor
C5, C6	0.1-μF capacitor
R1	100-kΩ, 1/4-W, 5% resistor
R2	47-kΩ, 1/4-W, 5% resistor
R3	82-kΩ, 1/4-W, 5% resistor
R4	220-kΩ, 1/4-W, 5% resistor
R5–R8	330-Ω, 1/4-W, 5% resistor

stage generates an output frequency of about:

$$F = \frac{1}{0.693 \times 0.000025 \times [82,000 + (2 \times 220,000)]}$$
$$= \frac{1}{0.693 \times 0.000025 \times (82,000 + 440,000)}$$
$$= \frac{1}{0.693 \times 0.000025 \times 522,000}$$
$$= \frac{1}{9.04}$$
$$= 0.11 \text{ Hz}$$

The output signals from the two astable multivibrators are fed through a digital-gating network (IC2 and IC3) and fed out through four separate outputs. Each output drives its own individual LED (D1 through D4). When a given output goes high, its LED lights up, otherwise, that particular LED is dark.

Each output combines the two signal frequencies in a different way. The truth table for output 1 is:

Inputs	Output
A B	
L L	H
L H	L
H L	L
H H	L

LED D1 is lit only when both multivibrators are currently putting out a low signal.

The truth table for output 2 is:

Inputs	Output
A B	
L L	L
L H	L
H L	H
H H	L

LED D2 is dark except when multivibrator A is putting out a high signal while multivibrator B is simultaneously putting out a low signal.

The truth table for output 3 is:

Inputs	Output
A B	
L L	L
L H	H
H L	L
H H	L

LED D3 is lit only when multivibrator A is putting out a low signal while multivibrator B is simultaneously putting out a high signal.

Finally, the truth table for output 4 is:

Inputs	Output
A B	
L L	L
L H	L
H L	L
H H	H

LED D4 is lit only when both multivibrators are currently putting out a high signal.

As you can see, three of the LEDs are dark at all times, as long as power is supplied to the circuit. One, and only one, LED is lit at any given instant. The LEDs "take turns" lighting up in a complex, seemingly random pattern.

In experimenting with this circuit, you might want to try a few other digital gating networks.

Because CMOS digital gates are used in this project, the supply voltage should be suitable to these devices. A + 9-V supply is recommended.

PROJECT 37: RANDOM-NUMBER GENERATOR

The circuit illustrated in Fig. 4-9 can be used for games, ESP tests, or any other application in which random numbers are needed.

When pushbutton switch (S1) is closed, all ten output LEDs (D1 through D10) will appear to be lit continuously. (They actually are blinking sequentially on and off, but at a rate much too fast for the human eye to catch.)

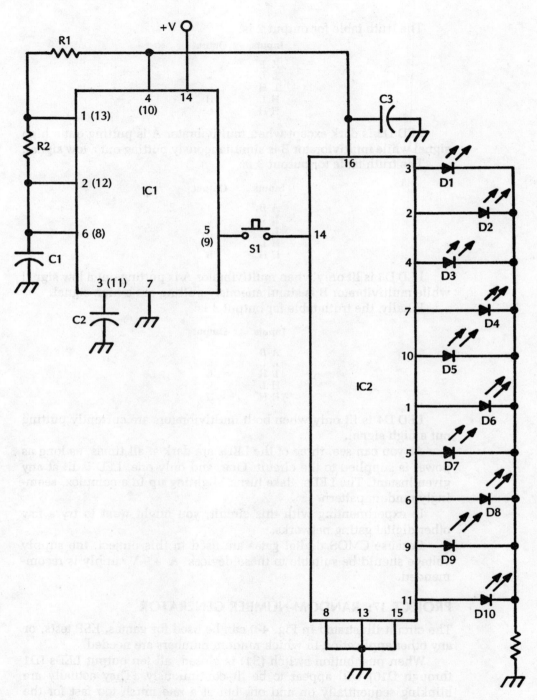

Fig. 4-9 *Project 37: Random-number selector.*

When the switch is released, one and only one of the LEDs will remain lit, and the other nine will go dark. There is no way to predict which LED will remain on when the switch is released.

Table 4-8 shows a suitable parts list for this project. There isn't much that is interesting to experiment with in this project.

**Table 4-8   Parts List for the
Random-Number Selector Project of Fig. 4-9.**

IC1	556 dual-timer
IC2	CD4017 CMOS decade counter
D1 – D10	LED
S1	Normally open SPST pushbutton switch
C1, C2	0.01-μF capacitor
C3	0.1-μF capacitor
R1	6.8k-Ω, 1/4-W, 5% resistor
R2	3.9k-Ω, 1/4-W, 5% resistor
R3	470-Ω, 1/4-W, 5% resistor

One-half of a 556 timer IC (IC1) is set up as an astable multivibrator. The other timer section is not used in this project. I suggest you build two of these circuits on the same board, increasing the random possibilities. You can use a DPST or DPDT pushbutton switch. When the switch is released, two LEDs will stay lit.

For the second timer section, use the pin numbers in parentheses for IC1. Of course, a separate CD4017 (IC2) must be used. All passive components (resistors and capacitors) in the circuit also must be duplicated.

To ensure variety in the two outputs, change the value of one or more of the timing components in the additional astable multivibrator stage (capacitor C1 and resistors R1 and R2). You don't want the two sections to be synchronized, or there would be no point at all in adding the second section.

The power supply for this circuit must be suitable for CMOS gates. I recommend a supply voltage of +9 V.

The astable multivibrator, or clock, must run at a fairly high frequency. The parts list uses the following component values:

$$C_1 = 0.01 \ \mu F$$
$$R_1 = 6.8 \ k\Omega$$
$$R_2 = 3.9 \ k\Omega$$

These components result in a clock frequency of approximately:

$$F = \frac{1}{0.693 \times 0.00000001 \times [6800 + (2 \times 3900)]}$$

$$= \frac{1}{0.693 \times 0.00000001 \times (6800 + 7800)}$$

$$= \frac{1}{0.693 \times 0.00000001 \times 14,600}$$

$$= \frac{1}{0.0001011}$$

$$= 9891 \text{ Hz}$$

There is no way you'll be able to distinguish the individual LED blinks at that rate.

When switch S1 is closed, the clock pulses drive the counter (IC2). When the switch is opened, the clock pulses no longer reaches the counter, so it stops at its last count value, lighting up the appropriate LED.

Because only one LED is ever illuminated at any given instant (even though they switch on and off at a very rapid rate), only a single current-limiting resistor (R3) is required in this project.

PROJECT 38: UP/DOWN FLASHER

Figure 4-10 shows a very unusual and sophisticated LED flasher circuit. This is one of the most sophisticated and complex circuits in this book. Fortunately, most of the work is done by four ICs. Table 4-9 shows the complete parts list for this project.

Note that three of the four ICs in this project are CMOS-type digital devices. The power-supply voltage should be selected accordingly. A good supply voltage for this circuit would be + 9 V.

If for some reason you cannot locate the 74C193 and the 74C154 chips called for in the parts list, you can substitute the following TTL ICs:

IC2	7400 or 74LS00
IC3	74193 or 74LS193
IC4	74154 or 74LS154

If TTL chips are used, the power supply for the circuit must be a well-regulated + 5 V. TTL gates are very fussy about their power-supply requirements. If you make one of these substitutions, make them all. Do not intermingle TTL and CMOS devices in this circuit.

Only one section of the 556 timer IC (IC1) is used in this circuit. If you prefer, you could substitute a 555 single timer, or you could use a 7555 CMOS timer, for an all-CMOS project. If you do use a 556 dual-timer chip, you can use the unused timer section in other circuitry to create a larger system of some sort.

There are 16 outputs from IC4. Each output drives its own individual LED. Only one LED will be lit at any given time. The other fifteen

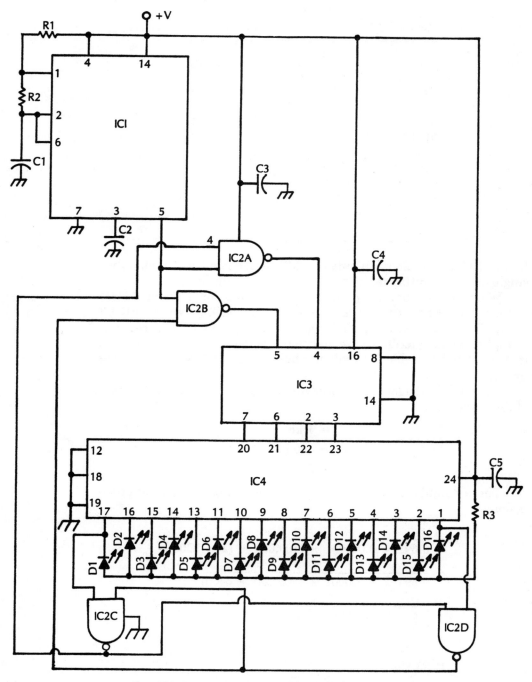

Fig. 4-10   *Project 38: Up/down flasher.*

**Table 4-9   Parts List
for the Up/Down Flasher Project of Fig. 4-10.**

IC1	556 dual-timer
IC2	CD4011 CMOS quad NAND gate (see text)
IC3	74C193 CMOS up/down counter (see text)
IC4	74C154 CMOS 4- to 16-line decoder (see text)
D1 – D16	LED
C1	1-μF, 35-V electrolytic capacitor
C2	0.01-μF capacitor
C3, C4, C5	0.1-μF capacitor
R1	100-kΩ, 1/4-W, 5% resistor
R2	2.2-kΩ, 1/4-W, 5% resistor
R3	390-Ω, 1/4-W, 5% resistor

LEDs will be dark. Because only one LED is activated at a time, only a single current-limiting resistor (R3) is needed in this circuit.

When power is applied to this circuit, it will count up from LED D1 to LED D16, then reverse direction and count back down to LED D1 again. This back and forth pattern repeats endlessly for as long as power is applied to the circuit. The sequence rate is determined by the output frequency of the astable multivibrator built around IC1, which serves as the system clock.

The parts list suggests the following component values for this part of the circuit:

$$C_1 = 1\,\mu F$$
$$R_1 = 100\text{ k}\Omega$$
$$R_2 = 2.2\text{ k}\Omega$$

These component values give you a clock frequency of approximately:

$$F = \frac{1}{0.693 \times 0.000001 \times [100,000 + (2 \times 2200)]}$$
$$= \frac{1}{0.693 \times 0.000001 \times (100,000 + 4400)}$$
$$= \frac{1}{0.693 \times 0.000001 \times 104,400}$$
$$= \frac{1}{0.072}$$
$$= 14\text{ Hz}$$

Each step in the sequence lasts approximately 3/4 second. This is how long each LED will stay lit before the circuit moves on to the next

LED in the sequence. It will take about 2¹/₄ seconds for a complete up/down count sequence. You can slow down the sequence by increasing the value of any or all of the timing components—capacitor C1 and resistors R1 and R2.

The brightness of the LEDs can be altered by changing the value of resistor R3. The smaller this resistance is, the brighter the LEDs will glow. Do not make this resistor smaller than 100 Ω, or the LEDs might be damaged by excessive current flow. At the other extreme, if resistor R3 is made larger than about 1 Ω it will be difficult, or possibly impossible, to tell which LED is lit. The glow will be too dim.

The remaining passive components in this circuit are all stabilizing bypass capacitors (C2 through C5). The values of these capacitors are not at all crucial, and do not directly affect the operation of the circuit, so there is no real point in experimenting with alternate values for these capacitors.

❖ 5

Miscellaneous projects

THIS FINAL CHAPTER IS A HODGEPODGE OF MISCELLANEOUS TIMER PROJECTS that don't quite fit into any neat chapter categories. Although some of these projects are not easy to classify, I think you'll find them interesting and worthwhile applications for the 556 dual-timer IC.

PROJECT 39: PULSED-RELAY DRIVER

The circuit shown in Fig. 5-1 is designed to activate periodically an electromechanical relay. The relay should be selected to suit the intended load. The required switch contacts for the relay will depend on your specific intended application. The relay also should be selected to be activated by the output voltage from the timer. When the output is high, this voltage will be a little less than the circuit's supply voltage (V+). In some applications, you might need to use an intermediate relay to drive a larger relay. The 555 (556) timer is generally sufficient to drive a small to moderately sized relay. Table 5-1 shows a suitable parts list for this project. You can experiment with alternate component values.

The first timer stage in this circuit is an astable multivibrator. The frequency, or pulse rate, is controlled by capacitor C1, resistors R1 and R3, and the setting of potentiometer R2. This potentiometer permits manual control over the pulse rate. If this feature is not appropriate for your particular application, you can combine R2 and R3 into a single fixed resistor.

Generally speaking, to drive a pulsed relay, the astable multivibrator stage should be set for a relatively low frequency, well into the sub-audio range. In most cases, a pulse frequency of considerably less than 1 Hz (one pulse per second) is appropriate, which requires rather large values for the timing components in this part of the circuit (C1, R2, and

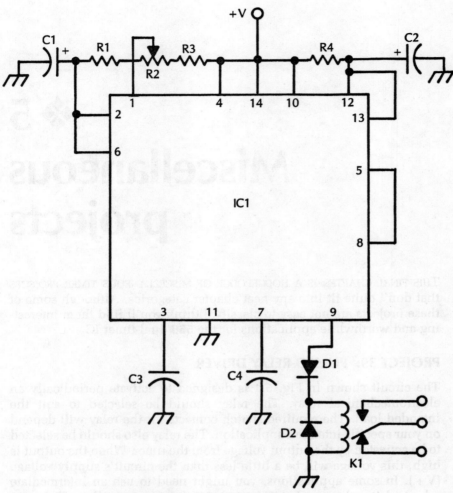

Fig. 5-1   *Project 39: Pulsed-relay driver.*

**Table 5-1   Parts List for the
Pulsed-Relay Driver Project of Fig. 5-1.**

IC1	556 dual-timer IC
D1, D2	Small signal diode (1N914, or similar)
K1	Relay (to suit load)
C1	250-µF, 35-V electrolytic capacitor
C2	25-µF, 35-V electrolytic capacitor
C3, C4	0.01-µF capacitor
R1	2.2-kΩ, ¼-W, 5% resistor
R2	500-kΩ potentiometer
R3, R4	100-kΩ, ¼-W, 5% resistor

R3). Resistor R1 usually will have a relatively small value (as compared to the series combination of R2 and R3) to generate fairly narrow pulses.

According to the parts list, the following component values are suggested for this portion of the circuit:

$$R_1 = 2.2 \text{ k}\Omega$$
$$R_2 = 500 \text{ k}\Omega$$
$$R_3 = 100 \text{ k}\Omega$$
$$C_1 = 250 \text{ } \mu\text{F}$$

Of course, you should select timing component values appropriate to your specific intended application for the circuit.

I will assume that the potentiometer (R2) is set precisely at its mid-point, which gives it a value of 250 k (250,000 ohms). This resistance is in series with resistor R3. Resistances in series add, so the combined value of R2 and R3 is:

$$R_s = 250,000 + 100,000$$
$$= 350,000$$

This gives the astable multivibrator portion of the circuit an output frequency of:

$$F = \frac{1}{0.693 \times 0.00025 \times [2200 + (2 \times 350,000)]}$$
$$= \frac{1}{0.693 \times 0.00025 \times (2200 + 700,000)}$$
$$= \frac{1}{0.693 \times 0.00025 \times 702,200}$$
$$= \frac{1}{121.6}$$
$$= 0.008 \text{ Hz}$$

With the component values suggested in the parts list, the circuit outputs a pulse about once every two minutes.

The output of the astable multivibrator stage drives a monostable multivibrator, using the other half of the 556. The time constant of the monostable multivibrator, and thus, the time the relay is held in its active state, is determined by the values of resistor R4 and capacitor C2. Once again, relatively large values usually will be called for in most practical relay applications.

The parts list suggests the following component values:

$$R_4 = 100 \text{ k}\Omega$$
$$C_2 = 25 \text{ } \mu\text{F}$$

This gives the monostable multivibrator a timing period equal to:

$$T = 1.1R_4C_2$$
$$= 1.1 \times 100,000 \times 0.000025$$
$$= 2.75 \text{ seconds}$$

If all of the parts values recommended in the sample parts list (Table 5-1) are used, the relay will be activated for $2^3/_4$ seconds approximately every two minutes. Of course other component values will alter these timing values.

Capacitors C3 and C4 are stabilizing bypass capacitors for the unused voltage-control inputs of the two timer sections of the 556 IC. The value of these capacitors is not at all crucial.

Diode D1 protects the relay coil from any possibility of a negative voltage. Diode D2 protects the coils against a surge of back-emf induced when the activating signal suddenly drops from high to low. Neither of these diodes requires any special characteristics. Almost any small signal diodes will do just fine. The 1N914 diodes suggested in the parts list are probably the most readily available signal diodes. The same diode type often is numbered 1N4148.

PROJECT 40: TIME-DELAY-RELAY DRIVER

The circuit shown in Fig. 5-2 is another relay driver project. In many ways it is similar to the circuit illustrated back in Fig. 5-1, except this circuit requires an external trigger pulse. After the trigger pulse is received, there is a fixed delay period before the relay is activated for a specific period of time.

Both timer stages in this circuit are used in the monostable mode. The first timer stage controls the delay period through the values of resistor R1 and capacitor C1. The second timer stage determines the length of the output pulse (how long the relay is activated) according to the values of resistor R2 and capacitor C2.

Table 5-2 shows a suitable parts list for this project. As I've suggested for most of the projects in this book, you can experiment with alternate component values in this circuit.

Once again, the relay you select should suit the individual requirements of your specific intended load. The required switch contacts for the relay will depend on your specific intended application. The relay should also be selected to be activated by the output voltage from the timer. This voltage, when the output is high, will be a little less than the circuit's supply voltage (V +). In some applications, you might need to use an intermediate relay to drive a larger relay. The 555 (556) timer is generally sufficient to drive a small to moderately sized relay.

With the component values suggested in the parts list, the first monostable multivibrator stage has the following timing components:

$$R_1 = 220 \text{ k}\Omega$$
$$C_1 = 100 \text{ }\mu\text{F}$$

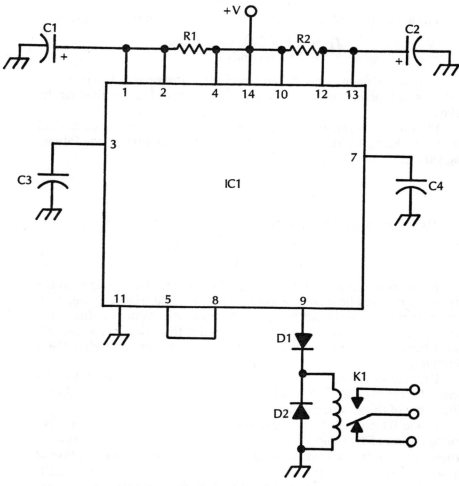

Fig. 5-2 *Project 40: Time-delay-relay driver.*

**Table 5-2   Parts List for the
Time-Delay-Relay Driver Project of Fig. 5-2.**

IC1	556 dual-timer IC
D1, D2	Small signal diode (1N914, or similar)
K1	Relay to suit load
C1	100-μF, 35-V electrolytic capacitor
C2	50-μF, 35-V electrolytic capacitor
C3, C4	0.01-μF capacitor
R1	220-kΩ, 1/4-W, 5% resistor
R2	330-kΩ, 1/4-W, 5% resistor

These components give this timer stage a timing period equal to:

$$T_1 = 1.1 \times 220,000 \times 0.0001$$
$$= 24.2 \text{ seconds}$$

This is the delay time. When the circuit is triggered, it will wait a little over 24 seconds before the circuit output goes high, activating the relay.

Similarly, the second monostable multivibrator stage is controlled by resistor R2 and capacitor C2, which the parts list assigns the following values:

$$R_2 = 330 \text{ k}\Omega$$
$$C_2 = 50 \text{ }\mu\text{F}$$

Therefore, the timing period for this stage works out to:

$$T_2 = 1.1 \times 330,000 \times 0.00005$$
$$= 18.15 \text{ seconds}$$

If the component values suggested in the parts list are used in the circuit, there will be a 24.2 second pause after the trigger pulse; then the relay will be activated for about 18 seconds. After this time, the timer circuit's output will go low, releasing the relay to its normal, deactivated state. Of course, other component values will alter these timings.

Capacitors C3 and C4 are stabilizing bypass capacitors for the unused voltage-control inputs of the two timer sections of the 556 IC. The value of these capacitors is not at all crucial.

Diode D1 protects the relay coil from any possibility of a negative voltage. Diode D2 protects the coil against a surge of back-emf induced when the activating signal suddenly drops from high to low. Neither of these diodes requires any special characteristics. Almost any small-signal diodes will do just fine. The 1N914 diodes suggested in the parts list are probably the most readily available signal diodes. The same diode type often is numbered 1N4148. Such protective diodes are highly recommended in any relay circuit to protect the delicate wires used in the coil winding.

PROJECT 41: RANDOM-VOLTAGE GENERATOR

In some specialized applications, you might need a random (or quasi-random) control voltage, which varies over time. One approach to this goal appears in Fig. 5-3. Four 555-type astable multivibrators are used to generate a complex, quasi-random pattern of voltages. Table 5-3 shows a suggested parts list for this project.

This project uses two dual-timer ICs. Each timer stage is wired as a very low-frequency astable multivibrator.

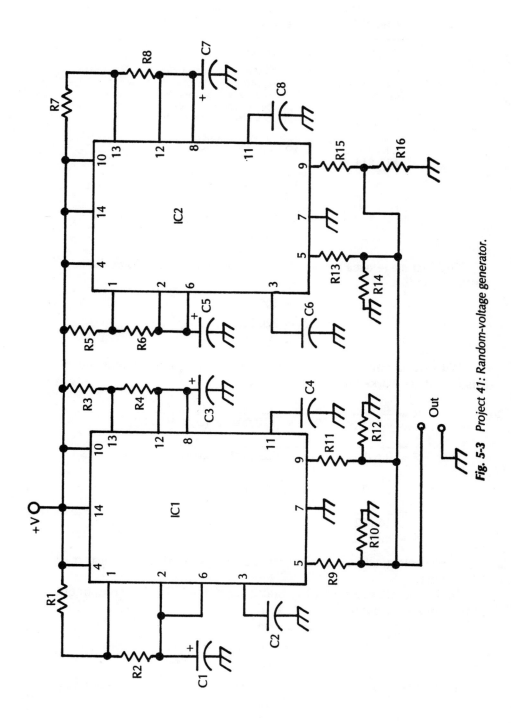

Fig. 5-3 *Project 41: Random-voltage generator.*

**Table 5-3 Parts List for the
Random-Voltage Generator Project of Fig. 5-3.**

IC1, IC2	556 dual-timer
C1	100-μF, 35-V electrolytic capacitor
C2, C4, C6, C8	0.01-μF capacitor
C3	220-μF, 35-V electrolytic capacitor
C5	330-μF, 35-V electrolytic capacitor
C7	500-μF, 35-V electrolytic capacitor
R1, R5	220-kΩ, 1/4-W, 5% resistor
R2, R4, R9, R10, R12, R14, R16	10-kΩ, 1/4-W, 5% resistor
R3, R7	100-kΩ, 1/4-W, 5% resistor
R6, R8	22-kΩ, 1/4-W, 5% resistor
R11	27-kΩ, 1/4-W, 5% resistor
R13	47-kΩ, 1/4-W, 5% resistor
R15	68-kΩ, 1/4-W, 5% resistor

The first stage uses the following component values from the suggested parts list:

$$C_1 = 100 \ \mu F$$
$$R_1 = 220 \ k\Omega$$
$$R_2 = 10 \ k\Omega$$

With these component values, the signal frequency generated by this first stage works out to:

$$
\begin{aligned}
F &= \frac{1}{0.693 \times 0.0001 \times [220,000 + (2 \times 10,000)]} \\
&= \frac{1}{0.693 \times 0.0001 \times (220,000 + 20,000)} \\
&= \frac{1}{0.693 \times 0.0001 \times 240,000} \\
&= \frac{1}{16.632} \\
&= 0.06 \ Hz
\end{aligned}
$$

Each cycle generated by the first timer stage in this circuit lasts over 16 seconds.

In the second astable multivibrator stage, the following component values are recommended:

$$C_3 = 220 \ \mu F$$
$$R_3 = 100 \ k\Omega$$
$$R_4 = 10 \ k\Omega$$

With these component values, the signal frequency generated by this second stage works out to:

$$F = \frac{1}{0.693 \times 0.00022 \times [100,000 + (2 \times 10,000)]}$$
$$= \frac{1}{0.693 \times 0.00022 \times (100,000 + 20,000)}$$
$$= \frac{1}{0.693 \times 0.00022 \times 120,000)}$$
$$= \frac{1}{18.295}$$
$$= 0.055 \text{ Hz}$$

Each cycle generated by the first timer stage in this circuit lasts just over 18 seconds.

You will be using the following component values in the third astable multivibrator stage:

$$C_5 = 330 \ \mu F$$
$$R_5 = 220 \ k\Omega$$
$$R_6 = 22 \ k\Omega$$

With these component values, the signal frequency generated by this third stage works out to:

$$F = \frac{1}{0.693 \times 0.00033 \times [220,000 + (2 \times 22,000)]}$$
$$= \frac{1}{0.693 \times 0.00033 \times (220,000 + 44,000)}$$
$$= \frac{1}{0.693 \times 0.00033 \times 264,000}$$
$$= \frac{1}{60.374}$$
$$= 0.017 \text{ Hz}$$

Each cycle generated by the first timer stage in this circuit lasts slightly more than a minute.

For the fourth and final astable multivibrator stage in this circuit, the following component values are suggested in the parts list:

$$C_7 = 500 \ \mu F$$
$$R_7 = 100 \ k\Omega$$
$$R_8 = 22 \ k\Omega$$

With these component values, the signal frequency generated by this final stage works out to:

$$F = \frac{1}{0.693 \times 0.0005 \times [100,000 + (2 \times 22,000)]}$$

$$= \frac{1}{0.693 \times 0.0005 \times (100,000 + 44,000)}$$

$$= \frac{1}{0.693 \times 0.0005 \times 144,000}$$

$$= \frac{1}{49.896}$$

$$= 0.02 \text{ Hz}$$

Each output pulse cycle from the fourth timer stage lasts slightly under 50 seconds.

Feel free to experiment with alternate timing component values in each of the four astable multivibrator stages in this circuit. For most practical applications, very low frequencies should be used, so fairly large component values will be called for.

The only restriction to the frequencies used in each of the four timer stages is that they should not be harmonics, or exact multiples, of one another. That is, if stage 1 is putting out a signal at 0.02 Hz, don't set up another stage to generate 0.01 Hz, or 0.04 Hz. The circuit will work if harmonic frequencies are used, but the result won't be very random or particularly interesting.

The output signals from each of the four astable multivibrator stages are passed through resistive voltage-divider networks composed of resistors R9 through R16. The dropped voltages then are combined at the circuit output. Each time one of the four astable multivibrator stages changes its state from high to low or from low to high, the output voltage will change. Different resistances are used in the four voltage dividers to give different "weighting" values to each of the component signals.

In each case, when a given signal is low, its voltage is effectively zero. A high output from a 556 or 555 timer is just slightly under the circuit's supply voltage. The voltage-divider networks drop the high voltage down to a lower level. For convenience in this discussion, I will assume that the supply voltage for the circuit is + 12 V, and a high signal reaches the full supply voltage value.

The first stage uses resistors R9 and R10, which both have suggested values of 10 kΩ. Obviously, the voltage at the midpoint between these two resistors will be one-half of the original voltage (+ 12 V), or:

$$V_a = \frac{V+}{2}$$

$$= \frac{12}{2}$$

$$= 6 \text{ V}$$

In the second stage, the voltage divider is made up of the following resistors:

$$R_{11} = 27 \text{ k}\Omega$$

$$R_{12} = 10 \text{ k}\Omega$$

The total resistance in the network is equal to the sum of the two component resistances:

$$R_t = R_{11} + R_{12}$$
$$= 27,000 + 10,000$$
$$= 37,000 \ \Omega$$

You can now use Ohm's Law to calculate the current flow through the two resistors:

$$I = \frac{V}{R}$$
$$= \frac{12}{37,000}$$
$$= 0.0003243 \ A$$
$$= 0.3243 \ mA$$

This means that the voltage dropped across resistor R11 must be equal to:

$$V_q = IR$$
$$= 0.0003243 \times 27,000$$
$$= 8.76 \ V$$

So the output voltage for the second stage works out to:

$$V_b = V+ - V_q$$
$$= 12 - 8.76$$
$$= 3.24 \ V$$

You can solve for the third stage's output voltage in the same way:

$$R_{13} = 47 \ k\Omega$$
$$R_{14} = 10 \ k\Omega$$
$$R_t = R_{13} + R_{14}$$
$$= 47,000 + 10,000$$
$$= 57,000 \ \Omega$$
$$I = \frac{12}{57,000}$$
$$= 0.0002105 \ A$$
$$= 0.21 \ mA$$
$$V_q = 0.0002105 \times 47,000$$
$$= 9.89 \ V$$
$$V_c = 12 - 9.89$$
$$= 2.11 \ V$$

Finally, you can use the same techniques to solve for the output voltage from the fourth and final stage in the circuit:

$$R_{15} = 68 \ k\Omega$$
$$R_{16} = 10 \ k\Omega$$

$$R_t = 68{,}000 + 10{,}000$$
$$= 78{,}000 \ \Omega$$

$$I = \frac{12}{78{,}000}$$
$$= 0.00015 \ \text{A}$$
$$= 0.15 \ \text{mA}$$

$$V_q = 0.00015 \times 68{,}000$$
$$= 10.46 \ \text{V}$$

$$V_d = 12 - 10.46$$
$$= 1.54 \ \text{V}$$

As each multivibrator stage goes high, it adds its weighted voltage to the output voltage. A low signal adds zero.

In this circuit, there are 16 possible combinations, which will be generated in a complex pattern. Each combination results in a distinct output voltage (see Table 5-4).

Table 5-4 Possible Combinations for the Random-Voltage Generator.

Stage State				Stage Voltages				Output Voltage
A	B	C	D	V_a	V_b	V_c	V_d	
L	L	L	L	0	0	0	0	0
L	L	L	H	0	0	0	1.54	1.54
L	L	H	L	0	0	2.11	0	2.11
L	L	H	H	0	0	2.11	1.54	3.62
L	H	L	L	0	3.24	0	0	3.24
L	H	L	H	0	3.24	0	1.54	4.78
L	H	H	L	0	3.24	2.11	0	5.35
L	H	H	H	0	3.24	2.11	1.54	6.89
H	L	L	L	6	0	0	0	6.00
H	L	L	H	6	0	0	1.54	7.54
H	L	H	L	6	0	2.11	0	8.11
H	L	H	H	6	0	2.11	1.54	9.65
H	H	L	L	6	3.24	0	0	9.24
H	H	L	H	6	3.24	0	1.54	10.78
H	H	H	L	6	3.24	2.11	0	11.35
H	H	H	H	6	3.24	2.11	1.54	12.89

Because the four astable multivibrator stages are operating out of sequence and at differing frequencies, these output voltages can be generated in any order.

With the component values suggested in the parts list, each output voltage will be held for about 16 seconds before changing to a new value.

The even-numbered capacitors (C2, C4, C6, and C8) are stabilizing bypass capacitors for the unused voltage-control inputs on the timers. Actually, in this particular application, you might want to eliminate the bypass capacitors. If any instability crept into this circuit, it would just make the effect a little more random, which would be just fine for this project.

PROJECT 42: THEREMIN

A *theremin* is a very unusual musical instrument. You play it without touching it. In the original theremin, a pair of antenna plates were used. The player waved his hands near the plates, producing different sounds.

In the simple theremin circuit illustrated in Fig. 5-4, photoresistors (R1 and R3) are used in place of the antenna plates. The player waves his hands over the photoresistors, casting varying shadows, altering the timing resistances in the circuit, and, thus, producing different sounds. Table 5-5 shows a suitable parts list for this project.

This project is quite simple. You just have two astable multivibrator stages. The first stage operates at a low (subaudible) frequency and modulates the second stage through the voltage-control input (pin #11).

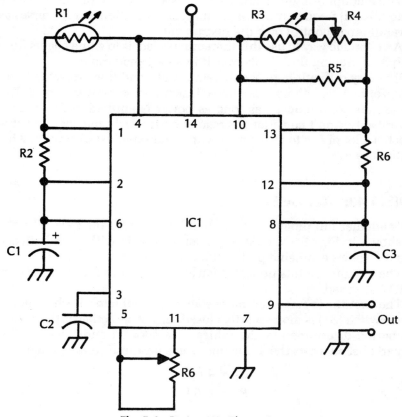

Fig. 5-4 Project 42: Theremin.

**Table 5-5   Parts List
for the Theremin Project of Fig. 5-4.**

IC1	556 dual-timer
C1	10-μF, 35-V electrolytic capacitor
C2	0.01-μF capacitor
C3	0.05-μF capacitor
R1, R3	Photoresistor
R2	47-kΩ, 1/4-W, 5% resistor
R4	1-MΩ potentiometer
R5	220-kΩ, 1/4-W, 5% resistor
R6	1-kΩ, 1/4-W, 5% resistor

Potentiometer R6 permits manual control over the depth of the modulation effect. The amount of light striking photoresistor R1 determines the modulation frequency.

The second astable multivibrator stage generates the actual audio-frequency tone. The actual frequency will vary in response to the modulation signal, of course.

The amount of light striking photoresistor R3 determines the base (unmodulated) frequency of the output tone. Potentiometer R4 serves as an overall range control over the instrument.

An alternate way to use this theremin project is to shine beams from a couple of moving flashlights over it in a darkened room.

It is very difficult to play a theremin well, and this project is fairly crude. For instance, there is no way to insert a pause between notes. The tone sounds continuously, as long as power is applied to the circuit. You probably won't consider the results particularly musical, but this project is a lot of fun to experiment with, and even just play with. Kids usually love it.

PROJECT 43: TOY LASER

Here's another fun project you can build as a toy for the kids. The circuit shown in Fig. 5-5 simulates a laser, complete with sound effects. Table 5-6 shows a suitable parts list for this project.

The circuitry in this project is fairly simple. Four timer stages (two 556 ICs) are used.

The first timer stage is a monostable multivibrator. Each time the trigger switch (S1) is momentarily closed, this stage activates the circuit for a period determined by the values of resistor R1 and capacitor C1. The parts list suggests the following values for these components:

$$C_1 = 4 \, \mu F$$
$$R_1 = 470 \, k\Omega$$

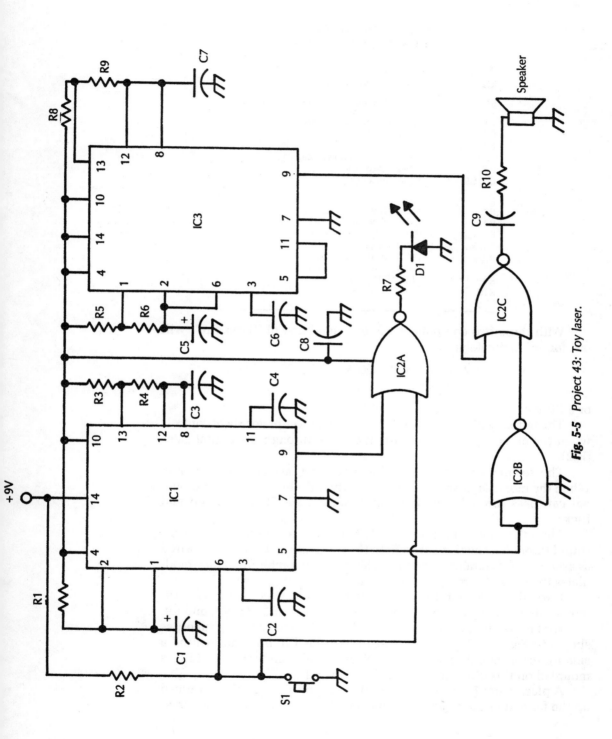

Fig. 5-5 Project 43: Toy laser.

**Table 5-6   Parts List for the
Toy Laser Project of Fig. 5-5.**

IC1, IC3	556 dual-timer
IC2	CD4001 quad NOR gate
S1	Normally open SPST pushbutton switch
C1	5-μF, 35-V electrolytic capacitor
C2, C4, C6	0.01-μF capacitor
C3	10-μF, 35-V electrolytic capacitor
C5	2.2-μF, 35-V electrolytic capacitor
C7	0.05-μF capacitor
C8, C9	0.1-μF capacitor
R1	470-kΩ, 1/4-W, 5% resistor
R2	1-MΩ, 1/4-W, 5% resistor
R3	10-kΩ, 1/4-W, 5% resistor
R4	100-kΩ, 1/4-W, 5% resistor
R5, R6	33-kΩ, 1/4-W, 5% resistor
R7	330-Ω, 1/4-W, 5% resistor
R8	47-kΩ, 1/4-W, 5% resistor
R9	1-kΩ, 1/4-W, 5% resistor
R10	100-Ω, 1/4-W, 5% resistor

With these two component values, each burst of "laser fire" will last for approximately:

$$T = 1.1 \times 0.000005 \times 470,000$$
$$= 2.585$$

or a little over 2$^{1}/_{2}$ seconds.

The output pulse from this monostable multivibrator stage controls when the other signals in the circuit can get through the digital gates (IC2).

The second half of IC1 is a low-frequency astable multivibrator. When the monostable multivibrator is activated, this low-frequency signal can pass through gate IC2A and cause LED D1 to light up and flicker.

The other 556 dual-timer IC (IC3) generates a pulsating "laser" sound through a small speaker. Both timer stages on this chip are wired as astable multivibrators. The first astable multivibrator frequency modulates the second through its voltage-control input (pin #11).

If you don't care for the way the effect sounds, experiment with different values for capacitors C5 and C7, and resistors R5, R6, R8, and R9.

For best results, install the circuit in a pair of telescoping tubes, as shown in Fig. 5-6. The circuit board is mounted in one end, behind a small circular board that just fits upright inside the tube. The LED is mounted on this circular board, facing forward.

A plastic lens (such as from a child's magnifying glass) is mounted on the far end of the other tube. The smaller tube fits inside the larger

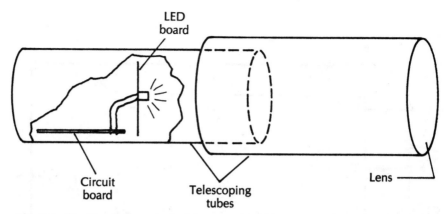

Fig. 5-6 *The Toy laser project of Fig. 5-6 should be mounted in a focusing tube.*

tube, and is moved back and forth to achieve the best focus. In a darkened room, you can see a narrow red dot where the "laser" hits its target.

The LED is slightly overdriven in this project to maximize its brightness. This will shorten its lifespan somewhat, but it should still hold up a fairly long time. I built my first prototype well over a year ago, and it still works fine.

PROJECT 44: ROULETTE WHEEL

Figure 5-7 shows yet another "fun and games" project. This circuit simulates the action of a roulette wheel. Table 5-7 shows a suitable parts list for this project.

If you cannot locate the CMOS 74C175 and 74C154 chips called for in the parts list, you can substitute TTL types (74175 and 74154). If TTL chips are used, the supply voltage must be a well-regulated +5 V. Both IC2 and IC3 should be the same logic family. Do not mix TTL and CMOS devices.

One-half of IC1 (the 556 timer chip) serves as a high-speed clock. When switch S1 is closed, the clock pulses drive the digital counter built around IC2. The counter, in turn, drives a 4- to 16-line decoder (IC3). When the push button is released (S1 is opened), no more clock pulses reach the counter, so one and only one of the 16 output LEDs remains lit. The LEDs should be arranged in a circular shape, like a true roulette wheel. The object of the game, of course, is to guess which LED will be lit when the pushbutton is released.

The other half of the 556 dual-timer IC is used to generate a clicking sound each time the count is advanced. This heightens the realism of the roulette-wheel effect. The clicks are produced through a small speaker. Capacitor C4 protects the speaker against any dc component in

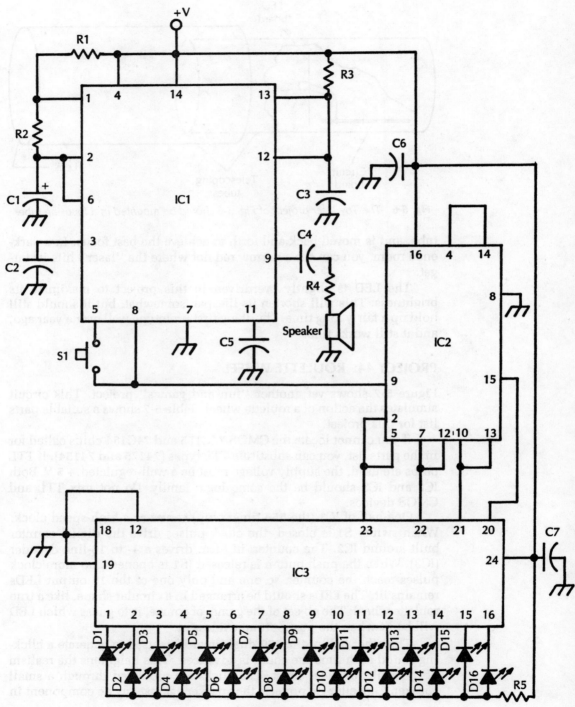

Fig. 5-7 Project 44: Roulette wheel.

**Table 5-7 Parts List
for the Roulette-Wheel Project of Fig. 5-7.**

IC1	556 dual-timer
IC2	74C175 quad-D flip-flop (see text)
IC3	74C154 4- to 16-line decoder (see text)
D1 – D16	LED
S1	Normally open SPST pushbutton switch
Spkr	Small speaker
C1	1-μF, 35-V electrolytic capacitor
C2, C5	0.01-μF capacitor
C3, C4, C6, C7	0.1-μF capacitor
R1, R2	47-kΩ, 1/4-W, 5% resistor
R3	1-kΩ, 1/4-W, 5% resistor
R4	100-Ω, 1/4-W, 5% resistor
R5	330-Ω, 1/4-W, 5% resistor

the output signal. The value of resistor R4 controls the volume of the clicks. You might want to consider using a potentiometer here.

For a more realistic effect, try feeding the output of a ramp-timer circuit (see chapter 2) to the control-voltage input of the first timer stage (pin #3). The clock frequency will gradually slow down, more accurately simulating the action of a mechanical roulette wheel.

PROJECT 45: ELECTRONIC DICE

The circuit shown in Fig. 5-8 is an electronic dice project. For most applications, you will want two dice. The part numbers in parentheses are for the second half of the circuit. Only half of the 556 dual-timer (IC1) and the hex inverter (IC3) are used in each half of the circuit, so these components do not need to be duplicated. The parts list for this project appears in Table 5-8.

When the switch is closed, the clock(s) (timers) advance the counter(s) (IC2 and IC5). The counters are arranged for six steps before recycling. IC3, IC4, and IC6 determine which LEDs are to be lit up for each count. When the switch is opened, the counting stops, and the current LEDs remain lit.

There are seven LEDs for each electronic die. They should be arranged in the pattern shown in Fig. 5-9. In this configuration, the lit LEDs will resemble the appropriate dice face patterns. The following LEDs are lit for each possible count value:

Count	D1	D2	D3	D4	D5	D6	D7
1	–	–	–	–	–	–	X
2	X	–	–	–	–	X	–
3	X	–	–	–	–	X	X
4	X	–	X	X	–	X	–
5	X	–	X	–	–	X	X
6	X	X	X	X	X	X	–

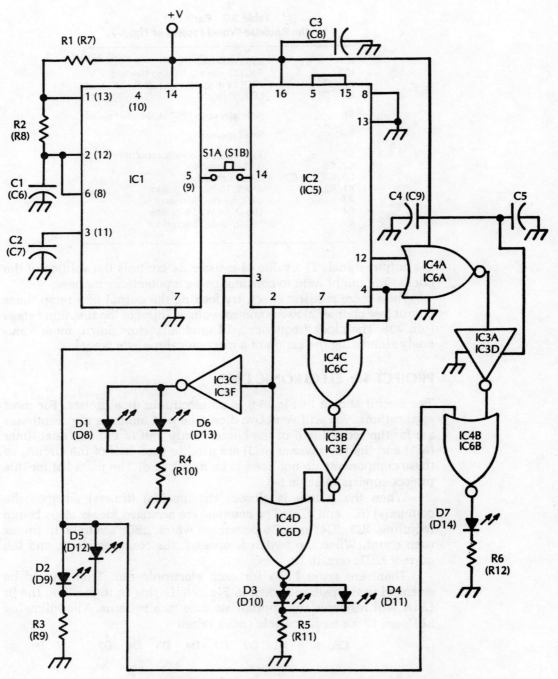

Fig. 5-8 *Project 45: Electronic dice (one-half circuit).*

**Table 5-8   Parts List
for the Electronic Dice Project of Fig. 5-8.**

IC1	556 dual-timer
IC2, IC5	CD4017 decade counter
IC3	CD4049 hex inverter
IC4, IC6	CD4001 quad NOR gate
D1–D14	LED
C1, C2, C6, C7	0.01-μF capacitor
C3, C4, C5, C8, C9	0.1-μF capacitor
R1, R2, R7, R8	1-kΩ, 1/4-W, 5% resistor
R3–R6, R9–R12	330-Ω, 1/4-W, 5% resistor
S1	Normally open DPST (or DPDT) pushbutton switch

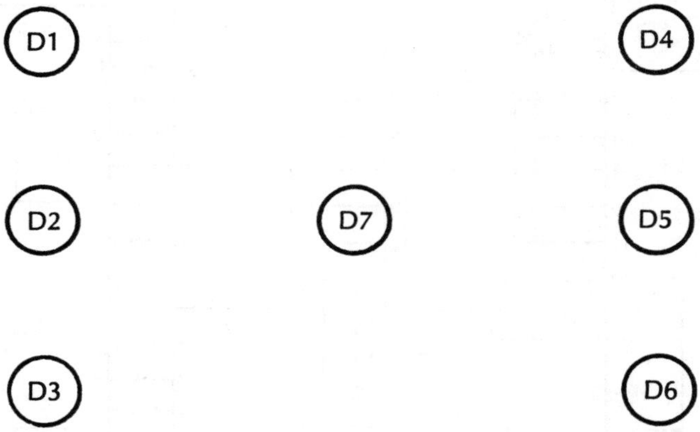

Fig. 5-9 *Seven LEDs arranged in this pattern can represent all six standard die faces.*

Note that certain LED pairs are always used in unison; when one is lit, so is its counterpart:

D1	D6
D2	D5
D3	D4

Note that separate clocks (timer astable multivibrator stages) must be used for both halves of the circuit, or both dice will always display the same value.

You can use the electronic dice in any game calling for regular dice.

PROJECT 46: MAGNETIC REED-SWITCH COUNTER

The circuit shown in Fig. 5-10 can be quite useful in surveillance and automation systems. This project is called a *magnetic reed-switch*

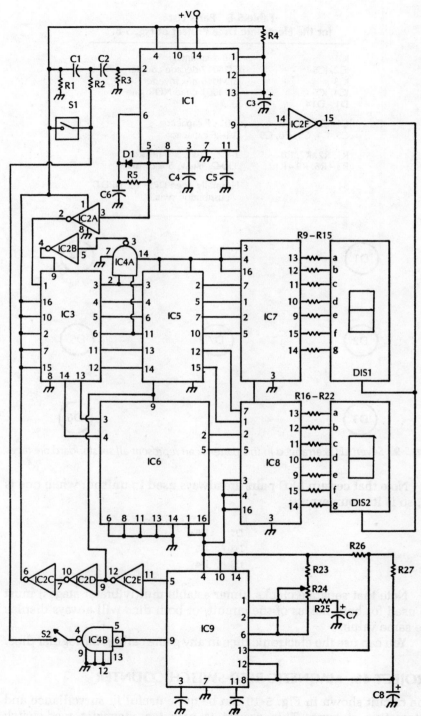

Fig. 5-10 Project 46: Magnetic reed-switch counter.

counter. The name is fairly self-explanatory. The circuit counts how many times a magnetic reed switch is activated.

Table 5-9 shows the parts list for this project. Don't be put off by the apparent complexity of the circuitry. Most of the work is done with the ICs. This is definitely one of the largest projects in this book, calling for nine integrated circuits, including two 556 dual-timer chips.

**Table 5-9   Parts List for the
Magnetic Reed-Switch Counter Project of Fig. 5-10.**

IC1, IC9	556 dual-timer
IC2	CD4049 hex inverter
IC3	CD4518 dual BCD counter
IC4	CD4011 quad NAND gate
IC5, IC6	74C174 hex D-type flip-flop
IC7, IC8	CD4511 BCD-to-7-segment decoder/driver
DIS1, DIS2	Seven-segment LED display, common cathode
S1	SPST magnetic reed switch
S2	SPDT switch
C1, C2, C4, C5, C6	0.01-μF capacitor
C3, C7	4.7-μF, 35-V electrolytic capacitor
C8	2.2-μF, 35-V electrolytic capacitor
R1, R3, R4, R5	1-MΩ, 1/4-W, 5% resistor
R2, R8, R25	1-kΩ, 1/4-W, 5% resistor
R6	47-kΩ, 1/4-W, 5% resistor
R7	2.2-kΩ, 1/4-W, 5% resistor
R9–R22	330-Ω, 1/4-W, 5% resistor
R23	100-kΩ, 1/4-W, 5% resistor
R24	500-kΩ potentiometer
R26	56-kΩ, 1/4-W, 5% resistor
R27	1.5-kΩ, 1/4-W, 5% resistor

A magnetic reed switch is a small enclosed switch unit that is activated only when it is in the presence of a sufficiently strong magnetic field. Magnetic reed switches are available in both normally open and normally closed configurations. The choice of which type to use would depend on the specific application you have in mind. For simplicity in this discussion here, I discuss only the normally open magnetic reed switch. The project could just as easily use a normally closed switch, but the response to the magnetic field would be reversed.

A switch is a switch, and it certainly is easy enough to count electronically the number of times the magnetic reed switch closes. (A switch-debouncing stage might be necessary in many practical applications.) In effect, you are counting how many times a magnet is brought near the magnetic reed-switch unit.

There are a great many potential applications for this project. For example, you could mount a permanent magnet on a revolving wheel or disc, so that it passes close to the magnetic reed switch once per revolution, as illustrated in Fig. 5-11. The counter circuitry will keep track of the number of revolutions of the wheel. By adding a timebase oscillator, you can determine how many times the wheel revolves per time period. If you combine this information with the known circumference of the wheel, you can determine its spinning speed. This concept could be used to construct an electronic speedometer for a bicycle, a go-cart, or even an automobile.

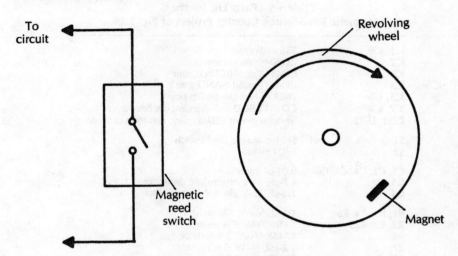

Fig. 5-11 *A permanent magnet on a rotating wheel can be used with a magnetic reed switch to count revolutions.*

To calibrate this type of speedometer, you must know the precise circumference (distance around the outermost edge) of the wheel. You then can calculate the revolutions for a given distance of travel.

Another possible application for a magnetic reed-switch counter is to measure wind speed. A wind vane with air-catching cups can be set up to turn a shaft with a magnet mounted on it. The digital circuitry then counts the number of shaft revolutions, or how many times the magnet moves past the magnetic reed switch.

Although the magnetic reed-switch counter circuit of Fig. 5-10 looks quite complex, it isn't very hard to follow its operation, if you break up the circuit into a functional block diagram, as shown in Fig. 5-12.

Each time the magnetic reed switch is closed, it triggers a monostable multivibrator, which functions as a switch debouncer. This signal is gated with a timebase oscillator and then is counted by a digital circuit. Because CMOS devices are used in this circuit, the supply voltage should be selected accordingly. A + 9-V supply is a good choice.

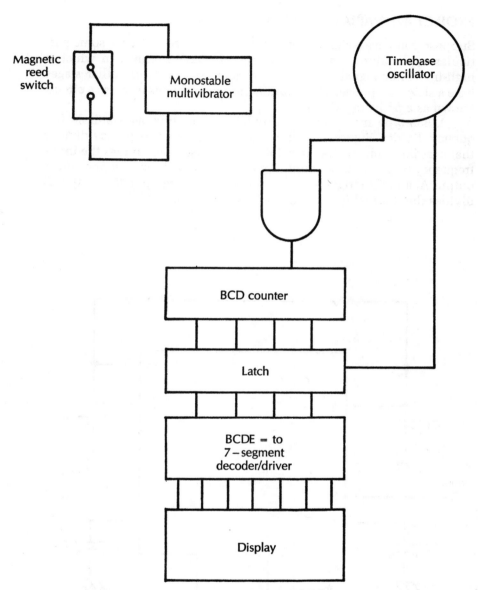

Fig. 5-12 *This is a block diagram for the Magnetic reed-switch counter circuit of Fig. 5-10.*

     The count value is displayed on a pair of seven-segment displays. Values from 0 to 99 can be displayed directly.

     Potentiometer R24 is used to calibrate the circuit's readout. Closing switch S2 puts the counter into a test/reference mode, so you can easily determine when calibration is required.

PROJECT 47: VARIABLE-FREQUENCY DIVIDER

Suppose you have a signal that is at too high a frequency for some particular application. This often happens in large systems, in which a high-frequency signal is required by some stages, while other stages have a slower response. The solution to such problems is to use a circuit known as a *frequency divider*.

A 555-type monostable multivibrator can serve as a simple frequency divider. Figure 5-13 shows a more versatile frequency divider that uses both timer stages in a 556 IC. The first stage divides the input frequency by a specific amount. This divided signal can be tapped off at output A, and also triggers the second stage (through pin #8). Output B divides the original input frequency even further.

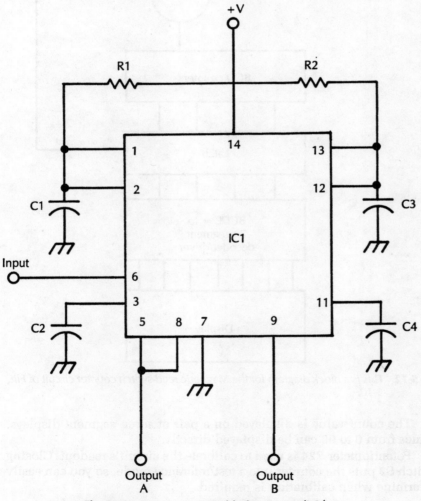

Fig. 5-13 *Project 47: Variable-frequency divider.*

The input signal is in the form of a string of pulses. One of the input pulses triggers the timer. Until it times out, the output is high. Once the timing period is over, the output will go low until the next input pulse is received.

A suitable parts list for this project appears in Table 5-10. The timing components (capacitors C1 and C3, and resistors R1 and R2) determine how the input frequency will be divided.

**Table 5-10   Parts List for
the Variable-Frequency
Divider Project of Fig. 5-13.**

IC1	556 dual-timer
C1, C3	0.1-μF capacitor
C2, C4	0.01-μF capacitor
R1	1-kΩ, ¼-W, 5% resistor
R2	2.2-kΩ, ¼-W, 5% resistor

PROJECT 48: FREQUENCY DIVIDER/PULSE SHAPER

Another variation on the basic frequency-divider circuit appears in Fig. 5-14. In this case, the second stage permits manual control over the duty cycle of the output waveform. Adjusting potentiometer R2 alters the output pulse width.

Table 5-11 shows a typical parts list for this project. You can experiment with alternate component values.

In this circuit, capacitor C5 is used to couple the output of the first timer stage to the trigger input of the second timer stage.

The actual frequency division works in the same way as in the preceding project. The input signal is in the form of a string of pulses. One of the input pulses triggers the timer. Until it times out, the output is high. Once the timing period is over, the output goes low until the next input pulse is received.

PROJECT 49: MISSING-PULSE DETECTOR

The final timer project in this book is the missing-pulse detector circuit shown in Fig. 5-15. A suitable parts list for this project appears in Table 5-12.

This circuit produces a negative-going pulse when it detects a gap, or one or more missing pulses, in a stream of pulses at the input. Missing-pulse detectors like this are used in continuity testers, communications systems, and security alarms, among other applications.

Note that only one timer section is used in this project. The other half of the 556 IC can be used in other circuitry in a larger system. Missing-pulse detectors are rarely used as "stand-alone" circuits.

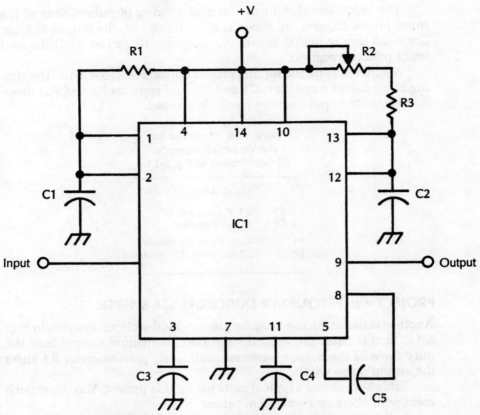

Fig. 5-14 Project 48: Frequency divider/pulse shifter.

**Table 5-11 Parts List
for the Frequency Divider/
Pulse Shifter Project of Fig. 5-14.**

IC1	556 dual-timer
C1, C2	0.1-µF capacitor
C3, C4	0.01-µF capacitor
C5	0.005-µF capacitor
R1	100-kΩ, 1/4-W, 5% resistor
R2	50-kΩ potentiometer
R3	10-kΩ, 1/4-W, 5% resistor

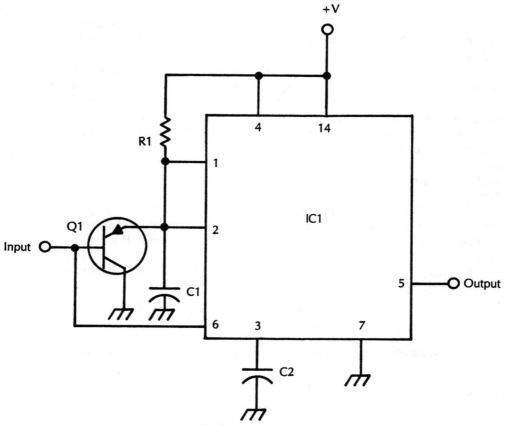

Fig. 5-15   *Project 49: Missing-pulse detector.*

**Table 5-12   Parts List
for the Missing-Pulse
Detector Project of Fig. 5-15.**

IC1	556 dual-timer
Q1	pnp transistor (2N3906, or similar)
C1	0.1-μF capacitor
C2	0.01-μF capacitor
R1	2.2-kΩ, 1/4-W, 5% resistor

Basically, this circuit is a monostable multivibrator that is continually retriggered by new pulses at the input before it has a chance to time out. Transistor Q1 adds this retriggering ability to the timer in this circuit.

Ordinarily, a new pulse is received at the input before the timer has finished its timing period. A new timing cycle is started by each input pulse. This can continue indefinitely as long as there is a steady, uninterrupted stream of input pulses. The output remains a constant high.

Now suppose that one of the incoming pulses is missing for some reason. The monostable multivibrator will now have a chance to time out, and the circuit output will go low until the input pulse stream starts up again. External digital circuitry can easily detect this condition.

You should select resistor R1 and capacitor C1 to give the desired timing period for your specific application. This timing period should be just slightly longer than the normal spacing between the input pulses.

The parts list suggests the following values for the timing components:

$$C_1 = 0.1 \ \mu\text{F}$$
$$R_1 = 2.2 \ \text{k}\Omega$$

With these component values, the circuit's timing period works out to:

$$T = 1.1 \times 0.0000001 \times 2200$$
$$= 0.000242 \text{ second}$$

These component values would be suitable if the input pulses normally have a frequency of about 4 kHz or so.

Capacitor C2 is a stabilizing bypass capacitor for the timer's unused voltage-control input. Transistor Q1 can be almost any low-power pnp device. The exact transistor type is not at all critical in this circuit.

Well, that's it. In this book you have worked with 49 practical applications for the 556 dual-timer IC. I'm sure you'll agree that this inexpensive and easy-to-use chip is a very versatile device. Now, what projects can you come up with on your own?

Index

Other Bestsellers of Related Interest

9 EASY ELECTRONIC PROJECTS FOR THE 747 DUAL OP AMP—Delton T. Horn

Explore the powerful 747 dual op amp as you experiment with these practical applications for this inexpensive, widely available, and easy-to-use workhorse circuit. You will find completely tested instructions for all the projects, including operational circuits, audio projects, signal generators, filters, test equipment, modulation projects, pulse circuits, and miscellaneous projects. 190 pages, 146 illustrations. **Book No. 3458, $15.95 paperback, $23.95 hardcover**

9 EASY ELECTRONIC PROJECTS FOR TRANSCONDUCTANCE & NORTON OP AMPS—Delton T. Horn

The projects cover a wide range of practical applications from dc amplifiers to current switches, voltage regulators to Schmitt triggers, and more. Each includes easy-to-follow instructions, and most can be constructed in a single evening costing less than $15 to build. Delton T. Horn gives you all the information you need to use transconductance and Norton op amps in your projects. 230 pages, 163 illustrations. **Book No. 3455, $16.95 paperback, $25.95 hardcover**

THE TALKING TELEPHONE—and 14 Other Custom Telephone Projects—Steve Sokolowski

Make an electronic lock that prevents unauthorized phone calls . . . add a music-on-hold adapter . . . make a phone "speak" numbers for the visually impaired . . . even burn a PROM for a character display. These easy and inexpensive projects let you totally customize your telephone. Many of these devices are exclusive to this book—you can't buy a commercially made version anywhere! 352 pages, 316 illustrations. **Book No. 3571, $17.95 paperback, $25.95 hardcover**

ALARMS: 55 Electronic Projects and Circuits —Charles D. Rakes

Make your home or business a safer place to live and work—for a price you can afford. Almost anything can be monitored by an electronic alarm circuit— from detecting overheating equipment to low fluid levels, from smoke in a room to an intruder at the window. This book is designed to show you the great variety of alarms that are available. There are step-by-step instructions, work-in-progress diagrams, troubleshooting tips, and advice for building each project. 160 pages, 150 illustrations. **Book No. 2996, $13.95 paperback, $19.95 hardcover**

ANALOG SWITCHES: Applications & Projects —Delton T. Horn

For more complex functions that demand speed and accuracy, an analog switch is essential. Delton Horn explains what analog switching circuits are an how you can put them to worthwhile use. Fifteen practical projects give you hands-on experience with the switching circuits presented. Easy to understand, this book is a valuable resource that contains all the information hobbyists, experimenters, and technicians need to build and modify their own analog switches. 160 pages, 114 illustrations. **Book No. 3445, $12.95 paperback, $21.95 hardcover**

THE COMPARATOR BOOK—with Forty-Nine Projects—Delton T. Horn

Horn sparks new interest in this low-cost device and offers hands-on applications as well as useful in-depth theoretical background. Step-by-step instructions, detailed diagrams, and complete parts lists are provided for each project. You don't have to be an expert, either. The projects gradually become more complex; those presented later in the book build on skills you developed while working on earlier ones. 200 pages, 155 illustrations. **Book No. 3312, $15.95 paperback, $23.95 hardcover**

CUSTOMIZE YOUR PHONE: 15 Electronic Projects—Steve Sokolowski

Practical, fun, phone enhancement projects that anyone can build. A melody ringer, an automatic recorder, and a telephone lock—these are just a few of the improvements you can add to make your everyday telephone more interesting and more useful. Steve Sokolowski explains the basics of constructing an electronic project as well as the fundamentals that make your telephone work. While the projects are all rather simple and inexpensive (built for about $10 to $30 each) they are also very useful. 176 pages, 125 illustrations. **Book No. 3054, $12.95 paperback, $19.95 hardcover**

Prices Subject to Change Without Notice.